Dorothy Parker's New York

Dorothy Parker aboard the SS *Normandie*, August 18, 1937, five days before she turned forty-four years old. *Source:* Dorothy Parker Society Archives.

Dorothy Parker's New York

Third Revised Edition

KEVIN C. FITZPATRICK

Cover Credit: © 2025 The Al Hirschfeld Foundation. All Rights Reserved.

Published by State University of New York Press, Albany

© 2025 State University of New York

All rights reserved. First published 2005. Second edition 2013. Third revised edition 2025.

Printed in the United States of America

No part of this book may be used or reproduced in any manner whatsoever without written permission. No part of this book may be stored in a retrieval system or transmitted in any form or by any means including electronic, electrostatic, magnetic tape, mechanical, photocopying, recording, or otherwise without the prior permission in writing of the publisher.

Links to third-party websites are provided as a convenience and for informational purposes only. They do not constitute an endorsement or an approval of any of the products, services, or opinions of the organization, companies, or individuals. SUNY Press bears no responsibility for the accuracy, legality, or content of a URL, the external website, or for that of subsequent websites.

EU GPSR Authorised Representative:
Logos Europe, 9 rue Nicolas Poussin, 17000, La Rochelle, France
contact@logoseurope.eu

Excelsior Editions is an imprint of State University of New York Press

For information, contact State University of New York Press, Albany, NY
www.sunypress.edu

Library of Congress Cataloging-in-Publication Data

Name: Fitzpatrick, Kevin C., 1966– author.
Title: Dorothy Parker's New York / Kevin C. Fitzpatrick.
Description: Third revised edition. | Albany : State University of New York Press, 2025. |
   Series: Excelsior editions | Includes bibliographical references and index.
Identifiers: LCCN 2024044694 | ISBN 9798855802375 (pbk. : alk. paper) | ISBN
   9798855802368 (ebook)
Subjects: LCSH: Parker, Dorothy, 1893–1967—Homes and haunts—New York (State)—New York. |
   Authors, American—Homes and haunts—New York (State)—New York. | Authors, American—
   20th century—Biography. | New York (N.Y.)—Intellectual life—20th century. | LCGFT: Biographies.
Classification: LCC PS3531.A5855 Z645 2025 | DDC 818/.5209 [B]—dc23/eng/20241004
LC record available at https://lccn.loc.gov/2024044694

To Christina

Contents

Acknowledgments	ix
Preface	xi
1. Dorothy Parker: A Manhattan Confection	1
2. An Apprenticeship in Cynicism: A Comfortable, Tumultuous Childhood	19
3. Drink and Dance and Laugh and Lie: The Vicious Circle Era	37
4. The Aisle Seat: Dorothy Parker as Theater Critic	69
5. Fighting for the Underdog: Activist	91
6. If You Can Get through the Twilight, You'll Live through the Night	109
7. Baltimore to the Bronx: The Epic Epilogue	119
Dorothy Parker Timeline	133
Notes	139
For Further Reading	143
Index	145

Acknowledgments

I thank the State University of New York Press for bringing out this "expanded edition" of a work that first was published in 2005 by Roaring Forties Press.

I also wish to acknowledge that this book would not be possible without Susie Rachel Baker, who introduced me to Dorothy Parker; the late Marion Meade; Roaring Forties Press publishers Deirdre Greene and Nigel Quinney, who published my first book; and the Rothschild family decedants Nancy Arcaro, Susan Cotton, and Joan Grossman. Special thanks to the Al Hirschfeld Foundation (David Leopold and Katherine Marshall-Eastman); Anthony Adams; Caitlin Bean; Richard Carlin; Les Dunseith; Todd Felton; Donald and Valerie Fitzpatrick; Allen Katz and the New York Distilling Company; Hannah Krasikov; The Lambs; the Long Branch Historical Association; Willis Loughhead and the staff of the Algonquin Hotel; Robert Mielke; Northeast Missouri State University; Darcie Hind Posz; Laurie Gwen Shapiro and *The New Yorker*, Stuart Y. Silverstein; Woodlawn Cemetery and Conservancy (Elizabeth Hunter, Susan Olsen, Barbara Selesky, Meg Ventrudo).

My deepest appreciation and love to my biggest supporters: my wife, Christina, and our son, Dylan.

Thank you all.

Preface

This is the expanded edition of my book, which was first published in 2005. Its roots go back to 1998, when I launched the website that became dorothyparker.com. That began two decades of researching the life and legacy of Dorothy Parker. In 2020 I carried her ashes from Baltimore to New York. It was an unimaginable experience to ride on Amtrak with a box I made myself in our basement, with Dorothy Parker's ashes riding next to me. As the train crossed from Maryland to Delaware, I poured myself a gin and tonic—mixing Dorothy Parker Gin, of course. I then buried her urn next to her parents in Woodlawn Cemetery, the Bronx.

Truly the honor of my lifetime was not only to be the one to shovel dirt onto Dorothy's new grave but also to design and help dedicate her gravestone in 2021.

I was incredibly blessed to meet Richard Carlin and learn that SUNY Press would bring out an expanded edition of *Dorothy Parker's New York*. For twenty years readers have enjoyed walking in Dorothy Parker's footsteps with my book. And now even more can follow her life from Manhattan to her final resting place.

I hope you will be entertained reading and carrying this book to explore New York. If you have a fraction of the fun I did while researching and writing it, you are in for a gloriously good time. I look forward to the day when readers bring this book from the Algonquin Hotel to Woodlawn Cemetery. Let the pages get wet with your gin stains as you carry a single red rose to her grave.

Kevin C. Fitzpatrick
Upper West Side
Summer 2024

1

Dorothy Parker

A Manhattan Confection

On February 6, 1965, Dorothy Parker took an ink pen in her seventy-one-year-old right hand and signed her last will and testament with her bold signature. *Dorothy* with a noticeable loop on the *D* was inked. Her signature matched her thirteen-year-old penmanship on 1906 postcards mailed to her father. A hapless forger in the 1990s attempted to match it.

Parker signed and initialed the four pages in her apartment inside the Volney Hotel, 23 East 74th Street, one block east of Central Park. The semiretired writer was clear in her intent to leave *everything* to Dr. Martin Luther King, Jr. She wanted no funeral or memorial service. However, there was one sentence missing from the document. Her attorney, Oscar Bernstien, did not capture where Parker's cremains should be delivered upon cremation. Two years later, on June 7, 1967, Parker died in that apartment of heart disease. In March 1971 the estate was closed with the Surrogate's Court, New York County.

This omission in 1965, never clarified, would play out for the legacy of Dorothy Parker for more than fifty-five years. The ashes of Dorothy Parker would change hands *six times*. During the height of the COVID-19 pandemic, Parker's urn was interred next to her mother and father on the 127th anniversary of her birth on August 22, 2020. This was international news. Exactly one year later, Parker's gravestone was unveiled.

Dorothy Parker's hometown is New York City. *Dorothy Parker* can only mean one place. The same as Central Park, the Empire State Building, and the Yankees' interlocking

NY logo. However, from 1988 to 2020 her ashes were in Baltimore. For a writer who had been so intrinsically tied to New York City since World War I, it was puzzling and confounding to her surviving family, friends, and fans that her gravesite was in Maryland. She was a New Yorker. Dorothy Parker had to be in New York. In 1928 she wrote:

> It is sentimental or presumptuous or too, too whimsical, according to the way you look at it, but my feeling for New York is maternal. I know it is a bad, headstrong, selfish brat, and will undoubtedly let me die in the poorhouse; I know its manners are, at best, but company ones, and its ways have been picked up from no companions of my choosing; I have for it all the futile exasperation of the clinging, jealous, bewildered mother. I know its faults, backward and forward and all around. And nobody but me is going to say anything about them while I am in the room![1]

A guide to her life in New York can now be complete, from cradle to grave: from the Upper West Side street where she took her first steps, to the Midtown speakeasies, and finally to her gravesite in the beautiful Woodlawn Cemetery, the Bronx.

Girl of Gotham to Legend

Few other writers have portrayed any city with as much keen and insightful detail as Dorothy Parker did when writing of Manhattan. She belongs to an impressive club of New York City writers—James Baldwin, E. L. Doctorow, J. D. Salinger, Edith Wharton—native sons and daughters who evoke, through their work, a city that is as alive and vibrant today as when they penned their words. In Dorothy Parker's New York, the speakeasies are always hopping, the party is just beginning, and all the taxicabs hold couples on their way to an *affaire de coeur*.

Dorothy Parker herself was a Manhattan confection: equal parts bootleg scotch, Broadway lights, speakeasy smoke, skyscraper steel, streetcar noise, and jazz horns. She was a product of a city struggling economically but on the verge of enormous power and influence. Dorothy, the precocious offspring of a Jewish father and an Episcopalian mother, would not have been comfortable in turn-of-the-century Los Angeles, with its dirt roads and deplorable culture. Chicago at the time was a cow town, a place of stockyards, not sophistication. And puritanical Boston certainly had no room for the likes of her.

A Parker Portrait

Figure 1. Dorothy Parker in her Hollywood period. She moved to Los Angeles in 1934. *Source:* Dorothy Parker Society Archives.

In 1940, Pocket Books published *After Such Pleasures* in paperback. At the end of the collection of short stories, Dorothy Parker's editor added a brief biography and portrait of the author, then in her late forties:

"Dorothy Parker is slightly over five feet in height, dark, and attractive, with somewhat weary eyes and a sad mouth. Her favorite possession is Robinson, a dachshund. She is superstitious, pessimistic, hates to be alone, and prefers to be considered a satirist rather than a humorist. She usually writes in longhand, crossing out every other word in order to achieve the utmost simplicity; she tries to avoid feminine style. Being extremely near-sighted, she wears glasses when writing, but she has never been seen on the street with them. Ernest Hemingway is her favorite author—flowers and a good cry are reported to be among her favorite diversions."

Only New York—with its bustling, crowded streets and undisputed role as the center of American popular culture—could have nurtured Dorothy, providing her access to, and friendships with, some of the most important cultural figures of the time. The life of Dorothy Parker is inescapably intertwined with the New York she inhabited; likewise, popular perception of New York and its history have been shaped by the life she lived and the world she captured in print.

Nineties New York: A City in Upheaval

At the end of the nineteenth century, New York was poised on the edge of tremendous economic, social, and political change. Dorothy was born into that world on August 22, 1893, in West End, New Jersey, at her family's summer beach cottage. That summer a catastrophic economic collapse launched a five-year depression in the United States. By the fall of 1893, 141 national banks had failed, followed by savings and loan institutions, mortgage companies, and private investment banks. Layoffs happened at an astonishing rate and only worsened during the freezing winter.

The same month that Eliza Rothschild delivered Dorothy, Joseph Pulitzer's *New York World* announced a "war on hunger" and recounted tales of the indigent to its readers. Intrepid reporters Nellie Bly and Stephen Crane wrote first-person accounts of the city's downtrodden, including stories about mothers who couldn't feed their children and turned them out into the streets. While the Rothschilds slept soundly, Pulitzer's newspaper wagons prowled the streets, handing out free loaves of bread (an early use of the term *breadline* in action). The New York police canvassed homes door to door to assess the alarming situation, reporting 70,000 unemployed, of whom 25,000 were women. City officials offered little relief for the poor. City government, controlled by the corrupt Tammany Hall political machine, was starting to be overturned by the forces of good government, but it would take years for real moral and social reform to take effect. Against this backdrop, the population was exploding. In 1900 New York City had just over 3 million residents; in 1910, 4.8 million; by 1920, 5.6 million people; and in 1930, more than 7 million—a 133 percent increase in just thirty years.

Although Henry Rothschild, born to immigrant parents, may not have felt much affinity for the newcomers from Europe overflowing the tenements on the Lower East Side, the newly arrived masses provided a dependable workforce. Some went to work for his garment business; others were employed as the family's household help. Dorothy never described what it was like inside her father's factory, but the use of sweatshop labor was so widespread that the working conditions there were quite likely poor and the pay minimal. In response to the harsh conditions, New York City soon became a hotbed for labor reform, with workers striking and thugs (and policemen) beating those in the picket lines. Child labor was an important issue, and women held strikes to protest intolerable working conditions for garment workers.

4 | Dorothy Parker's New York

Figure 2. Members of the 1909 Labor Day parade in New York. It would take until 1916 for the first Child Labor Act to pass Congress. *Source:* George Grantham Bain Collection, Library of Congress, Prints and Photographs Division.

Women's rights, especially the right to vote, was another galvanizing issue of the day. When Dorothy was sixteen, more than twenty thousand New York women wage earners went on strike for almost two months, and as she entered the writing profession in her early twenties, the suffrage movement was advocating voting rights for women. In October 1917, tens of thousands of women marched in a New York City suffrage parade. In June 1919, Congress proposed the Fifteenth Amendment, giving all citizens the right to vote regardless of sex; ratification was completed on August 18, 1920. This was the world into which Dorothy Parker was born and from which she drew her inspiration. However, although she occasionally ventured into working-class lives with stories like "Clothe the Naked" and "The Standard of Living," she was much more at home chronicling the limited options available to middle-class women of the early twentieth century.

Following the death of her father in 1913, she spent more time with her siblings in her early twenties. She motored around California in 1914 with her close friend,

Connecticut socialite Frances H. Billings. The following year, Dorothy Rothschild appeared in the Hartford society pages in Frances's wedding party. Among the guests was the bride's cousin, handsome stockbroker, Edwin "Eddie" Pond Parker II. They shared an affinity for dancing and Broadway; Eddie was a fan of the *Follies*. He was a broker for Morton, Lackenbruch and Co., with offices in the Equitable Building. They married in July 1917. He promptly left to serve in the Great War as an ambulance driver in the U.S. Army; he was exposed to poison gas and near-constant enemy fire. When he had shipped overseas, his wife was a lowly staff writer in the employ of Condé Nast. When he returned home, two years later, Dorothy Parker was a rising star as Broadway's first female theater critic.

Her Verse, Her Voice

In her verse, women are more likely to have their hearts broken by men than men are likely to be left heartbroken by women. In her fiction, she used stock characters for her female roles: dumb-bell office girls, blushing new brides, flustered girlfriends, and society matrons who are small-minded or silly (and frequently both). Few of these women gain power or satisfaction from their interactions with the men in their lives. A poignant and powerful example is "Mr. Durant," written for *American Mercury* magazine in 1924. It's the tale of a loathsome middle-aged businessman who impregnates his twenty-year-old secretary. Dorothy's descriptions of the dress and mannerisms of the young female office worker are masterly for their portrayal from Mr. Durant's perspective: "When she bent over her work, her back showing white through her sleazy blouse, her clean hair coiled smoothly on her thin neck, her straight, childish legs crossed at the knee to support her pad, she had an undeniable appeal."[2] As a Center Street trolley takes Mr. Durant uptown to his wife and children, he considers the dilemma with a cold, detached practicality: "As he had often jovially remarked to his friends, he knew 'a thing or two.' Cases like this could be what people of the world called 'fixed up'—New York society women, he understood, thought virtually nothing of it. This case could be fixed up, too. He got Rose to go home, telling her not to worry; he would see that everything was all right. The main thing was to get her out of sight, with that nose and those eyes." The New York City of Dorothy Parker's imagination was one where women needed to be "fixed up" or simply removed from sight. Her fiction and poetry don't feature women transcending the roles that society had prescribed for them—none of her characters become powerful theater critics or social gadflies or Oscar-nominated Hollywood screenwriters.

Uncle Martin on the *Titanic*

Figure 3. Pier 54, West Street at West 13th Street. This is the last remaining portion of the Cunard-White Star Line pier. In 1912 the survivors of the RMS *Titanic* were brought here aboard the RMS *Carpathia*. *Source:* Photo by the author.

The sinking of the RMS *Titanic* in April 1912 had a huge impact on Dorothy Rothschild, who lost her uncle in the tragedy. Like his older brother, J. Henry Rothschild, Martin Rothschild was an executive in the garment business; their parents, Samson and Mary, were German immigrants who had settled in Alabama in the 1840s.

Martin and his wife, Elizabeth Jane Barrett Rothschild, lived just nine blocks from Dorothy and her father, at 753 West End Avenue (the home is gone today). The couple had no children. Henry was very close to his younger brother; Henry gave his Long Branch beach cottage—where Dorothy's mother, Eliza, died—to his brother. Dorothy was eighteen at the time of the ship's sinking.

Martin and Elizabeth had been first-class passengers onboard the *Titanic*. According to the *Encyclopedia Titanica*, after the ship hit the iceberg on the night of April 15, 1912, Elizabeth got into lifeboat no. 6 with twenty-two others while Martin stayed aboard the doomed ship: "After the collision steward Frederick Dent Ray saw Mr. Rothschild coming out of his stateroom on C deck. 'I spoke to him and asked him where his wife was. He said she had gone off in a boat. I said, "This is rather serious." He said, "I don't think there's any occasion for it." Then the two men casually walked up to A deck where Ray went to a lifeboat."

It's not known if Dorothy and Henry met Elizabeth and the other survivors when the *Carpathia* docked at Pier 54 on April 18, 1912. Dorothy, who mentioned her family members only briefly in her work, never wrote about the *Titanic*. She was certainly not averse to passenger ships and sailed to Europe several times (not on White Star Lines). Martin's widow erected a memorial to him in the mausoleum where she is interred at St. Mary's Cemetery, in Watkins Glen, New York. Martin also has a cenotaph with his grandparents in Union Field Cemetery, Ridgewood, Queens.

Today, the old Pier 54 is part of Hudson River Park and steamships are just a memory. The old sign is still faintly visible in the rust, WHITE STAR LINES barely legible. It forms the entrance to Little Island at Pier 55, a 2.4-acre man-made island that opened to the public in 2021.

Gin and Sin: Dorothy Records the Jazz Age

Dorothy Parker was at her tantalizing best when she wrote about the apartment houses, afternoon teas, bridge games, train stations, and saloons that made up her New York life. She populated these settings with the unfaithful husbands, drunken social climbers, dissipated lovers, and cowardly gentlemen she saw around her. Yet, the themes she worked and reworked continue to resonate today. Spouses are still unfaithful to each other; heartbreak and loss are forever part of the human condition; boneheaded bosses, insecure lovers, haughty neighbors, dull-witted children—no matter what decade these characters appear in, they will be understood. William Shakespeare had his conflicted princes, Parker her alcoholic debutantes, and both remain fresh and recognizable. For a writer with Parker's remarkable talents, New York provided plenty of characters for fiction and poetry: bootleggers and stock traders, chorus girls and grande dames, Fifth Avenue swells, and the Bowery's down-and-outers.

The years of relative peace between World Wars I and II gave Parker the freedom to write about affairs of the heart, the trials of suburbia, the inanities of social convention, and even the merits of gin versus scotch—topics that in the hands of a trenchant observer such as herself not only made for timeless stories but, most importantly for her editors, sold magazines. The printed word was enjoying heady days when Parker's career took off. The city had at least fifteen daily newspapers, with editions rolling off the presses in the morning and afternoon. With the addition of scores of magazines and cheap pulps and hundreds of dime novels, sidewalk newsstands were bursting with titles.

Movies were still silent, radio was in its infancy, and live shows were the big thing at the city's nearly eighty Broadway theaters (today there are half that many). Parker began

8 | Dorothy Parker's New York

her career at *Vogue*, which had transformed itself from printing dressmaking patterns to dictating style. When she joined *Vanity Fair*—the magazine was just four years old and already the most sophisticated publication in the country—she was minted as the reigning arbiter of sass and class. Her snappy wisecracks (dutifully retold by her ink-stained chums) and mordant verse (sent in to the most popular daily newspaper columnists) made her a symbol of the roaring twenties and an expert on Broadway, banter, and bacchanalia.

Although she did not draw the intense media scrutiny attracted by a couple like Scott and Zelda Fitzgerald, she was one of the best-known women of the time. Her reputation came primarily from her wisecracks and prose "squibs," as she called them, but also from her short fiction. Her first book, *Enough Rope*, was a bestseller, going through eleven printings in fifteen months. At one point she was so famous that people followed her around waiting for her to say something funny; even worse, complete strangers accosted her, begging for a joke. Luckily, she was often up to the task. A woman at a party asked if she was Dorothy Parker.[3] "Yes, do you mind?" was her quick reply.

In a 1956 interview with the *Paris Review*—the only serious literary question-and-answer session she ever sat for—Parker recalled, "Why, it got so bad that they began to laugh before I opened my mouth."

Much of Dorothy's humor relied on satire. Her keen eye for socially damning detail was evident in the very first poem she sold, a thirty-six-line piece she submitted to *Vanity Fair* in 1915, called "Any Porch."[4] She was paid the sum of twelve dollars, more than a week's salary at the time (about $360 today). The poem, with its rhyming iambic couplets of droll dialogue, provided New York with its first taste of Dorothy Rothschild's ability to carefully observe and devastatingly mock the vapid inanities of the socialites who brushed up against her world. An excerpt:

"I'm reading that new thing of Locke's—
    So whimsical, isn't he? Yes—"
"My dear, have you seen those new smocks?
    They're nightgowns—no more, and no less."

"I don't call Mrs. Brown *bad*,
    She's *un*-moral, dear, not *im*moral—"
"Well really, it makes me so mad
    To think what I paid for that coral!"

"My husband says, often, 'Elsie,
    You feel things too deeply, you do—"
"Yes, forty a month, if you please,
    Oh, servants impose on *me*, too."[5]

Dorothy drew inspiration from what she witnessed in her social and professional life. She mimicked the language she heard and lampooned her hosts and companions in brilliant stories and clever verse. She was one of the first contributors to *The New Yorker* and had much to do with its rise in prestige. Yet, stories such as "Dialogue at Three in the Morning" and "Arrangement in Black and White" satirized the very readers the new magazine was cultivating.

A Place at the Table: The Vicious Circle

Though she skewered her friends and enemies, there were a few other New Yorkers with a sensibility akin to Dorothy's, and they soon found a common meeting ground. Just as one cannot think of mixing a proper martini without dry vermouth, Dorothy Parker's story cannot be served without acknowledging her membership in the Algonquin Round Table. This gathering of misfits and cutups—columnists, editors, press agents, writers—wrote itself into American popular culture in the twenties by living the Jazz Age lifestyle and reporting that life to their audiences. They typified, for many, a Manhattan of late nights in theaters, early mornings at house parties and speakeasies, long lunches, and a small bit of work squeezed in somewhere.

The group started meeting in June 1919, when the Algonquin Hotel hosted a welcome-home luncheon roast in honor of Alexander Woollcott, the *New York Times* drama critic, who had recently returned from two years in France as an enlisted man in the Great War. Although Dorothy produced much of her finest and most enduring work during this manic decade, it was her connection to the Round Table that made her a popular cultural icon of the Jazz Age. The group was practically inseparable, and with so many newspaper writers among them, their comings and goings were reported in the daily columns. On many afternoons, Dorothy might be the only female present, and her circle of friends could always count on her to say something wryly amusing.

You Might as Well Live

Beyond her daily lunches at the Algonquin Hotel, Dorothy Parker's private life was rocky and provided a seemingly endless source of material for her fiction, poems, screenplays, and plays. During the Round Table years, she had several breakups and reconciliations with her first husband, Eddie Parker. The estrangement caused by the recurring absence of Eddie (and, some twenty-five years later, her second husband, Alan Campbell) due to wartime service shows up in her 1943 short story "The Lovely Leave." The growing distance between Eddie and Dorothy, psychologically and physically, contributed to their divorce in 1928. Dorothy also had a string of love affairs, often ending in disaster.

By the time she was forty, she had tried to take her own life at least three times, often as a result of her loneliness. As Dorothy's many relationships foundered, she solidified a lifelong preoccupation with death. This fascination is perhaps understandable since she had lost her mother, stepmother, father, and a favorite uncle all before she turned twenty-one. Throughout her adult life, death was never far from her thoughts. The very titles of her books hint at death: *Enough Rope*, *Sunset Gun*, *Death and Taxes*, *Laments for the Living*. Images of death and burial appear repeatedly in her work. She even subscribed to undertakers' trade journals while working at *Vanity Fair* and wore tuberose (*agave amica*), an overpowering scent favored for dressing corpses.

Romantic misadventures and the ongoing flirtation with suicide that they inspired accentuated her sense of death's omnipresence. When she wrote her O. Henry Award–winning short story "Big Blonde" in 1928, she had already attempted suicide twice. This may explain why Hazel Morse, the tragic protagonist of the story, reflects, "The thought of death came and stayed with her and lent her a sort of drowsy cheer. It would be nice, nice and restful, to be dead." For Parker, life was not sacred and untouchable, as she commented in 1928's "Coda":

> There's little in taking or giving,
>   There's little in water or wine;
> This living, this living, this living
>   Was never a project of mine.
> Oh, hard is the struggle, and sparse is
>   The gain of the one at the top,
> For art is a form of catharsis,
>   And love is a permanent flop,
> And work is the province of cattle,
>   And rest's for a clam in a shell,
> So I'm thinking of throwing the battle—
>   Would you kindly direct me to hell?[6]

Dorothy's best defense against the darkness and sadness pervading her life was to attack; she built her reputation by using humor to defuse heartache and loneliness as much as to skewer social pretensions and emotional shallowness. Her most famous 1920s poems about death, desire, and love can be found today driving social media accounts and trips to tattoo artists.

She could not afford to be all doom and gloom, however; Dorothy was a freelance writer dependent on publishing in general-interest magazines, and her editors paid her to amuse and entertain. Even though she completed less than eight years of formal education, quitting school at fourteen, she got by well enough to write for a pantheon of the best-edited American magazines, including *Vogue*, *Vanity Fair*, and *The New Yorker*, because she could produce sterling material with the best of them.

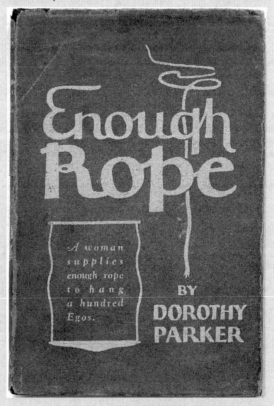

Figure 4. Boni & Liveright published Dorothy Parker's first book in 1926. It was a bestseller. *Source:* Dorothy Parker Society Archives.

Books Published during Parker's Lifetime

Dorothy Parker never wrote a novel or an autobiography. All of her books published during her lifetime were collections of pieces she wrote for periodicals, sometimes with unpublished poems included as well. The first three books she published were collections of poetry; when she had written enough short stories, these, too, were collected. After her death, other editions appeared. *The Portable Dorothy Parker* has stayed continuously in print since 1944; in 2006 it was expanded and revised.

COLLECTED POETRY

Enough Rope (1926)
Sunset Gun (1928)
Death and Taxes (1931)

COLLECTED POEMS

Not So Deep as a Well (1936)

COLLECTED FICTION

Laments for the Living (1930)
After Such Pleasures (1933)
Here Lies: The Collected Stories of Dorothy Parker (1939)

COLLECTED PROSE AND POETRY

The Portable Dorothy Parker (1944)

The Office

Her first job, working at *Vogue* for Condé Nast, paid her ten dollars a week. In her spare time she wrote and sold light verse to *Vanity Fair*, in the same building. Her big break came when she joined *Vanity Fair* and started writing drama reviews. With her byline becoming more common, she branched out into short fiction, selling pieces to the *Smart Set*, *American Mercury*, *The Bookman*, and *The New Yorker*. Eventually, she compiled her favorite pieces in single volumes, and those books quickly became bestsellers. And when Hollywood came calling, she went West and started pulling in big checks to put words in the mouths of actors for the early talkies. Her main audience throughout her career was women, and she got a lot of mileage—literally and figuratively—out of whom she called "the men I'm not married to."

No one, though, was safe; she could turn just as easily against her readers. Her subject might be the bore at the dinner party or the silly flapper on the street; she treated them all with a lacerating insight born of practiced cynicism. She particularly liked to adopt the air of the put-upon observer, such as in her "hate song" about women:

I hate Women.
They get on my nerves.

There are the Domestic ones.
They are the worst.
Every moment is packed with Happiness.
They breathe deeply
And walk with large strides, eternally hurrying home
To see about dinner.
They are the kind
Who say, with a tender smile, "Money's not everything."
They are always confronting me with dresses,
Saying, "I made it myself."
They read Woman's pages and try out the recipes.
Oh, how I hate that kind of woman.[7]

Parker wrote a series of these hate verses on such subjects as actors, men, her office, and wives, in which her powers of insight and observation sharpen her social commentary to a wicked-fine edge.

Dorothy and Religion

In the early 1900s, with the wave of immigrants hitting American shores—and particularly the streets of New York—came a growing awareness of the role of Jewish life in a modern America. She was raised as a WASP. Her mother was a Yankee; her father was Jewish but not observant, despite buying real estate among Jewish neighbors on the Jersey Shore and working in an industry—the garment trade—that had a long tradition with the religion. Dorothy's father enrolled her in a West 79th Street Roman Catholic elementary school, concealing her Jewish roots from the nuns. Perhaps Henry was merely following the traditional understanding of Jewish identity: A Jew is someone who was born to a Jewish mother or who converts to Judaism in accordance with Jewish law and tradition. Yet, when Dorothy reminisced about her time at the convent school, she referred to herself as a "little Jewish girl trying to be cute;" thus, at some level, she could not conceal her heritage from herself.

From an early age Dorothy saw religion, something others took so seriously, as both a burden and a farce. Where others turned to religion for comfort, she thought of God as the one who took away her mother and replaced her with an evil stepmother. Dorothy did not practice Judaism—or any religion, for that matter—at any time in her life. Her mother, stepmother, and both husbands were Christians, but her marriages were all civil ceremonies, and she claimed that one of the reasons she married Eddie Parker was for his "clean" surname, which she kept for the remainder of her life. While her stepmother, Eleanor, was fervently religious and demanded that young Dorothy say prayers at bedtime, a belief in God could not have been easy for this girl who had experienced so much loss at such a young age.

One wonders what the prayers of little Dorothy Rothschild were like. We can see Dorothy's unusual take on religion in "Prayer for a New Mother" (1928). The surprisingly tender ballad imagines the loss Mary must have felt after the Crucifixion:

The things she knew, let her forget again—
    The voices in the sky, the fear, the cold,
The gaping shepherds, and the queer old men
    Piling their clumsy gifts of foreign gold.

Let her have laughter with her little one;
    Teach her the endless, tuneless songs to sing,
Grant her her right to whisper to her son
    The foolish names one dare not call a king.

Keep from her dreams the rumble of a crowd,
    The smell of rough-cut wood, the trail of red,
The thick and chilly whiteness of the shroud
    That wraps the strange new body of the dead.

Ah, let her go, kind Lord, where mothers go
    And boast his pretty words and ways, and plan
The proud and happy years that they shall know
    Together, when her son is grown a man.

Although Parker certainly wasn't a regular at church or temple, her friends were aware of the mixed-religion no-man's-land of her childhood and teased her about it. When Aleck Woollcott taunted George S. Kaufman at the Round Table, bellowing, "You goddamn Christ killer," Kaufman defused the tension that his antisemitic friend had wrought by declaring with mock exaggeration, "For my part, I've had enough slurs on my race. I am now leaving this table, this dining room, this hotel, never to return." He paused to glance across the table at Mrs. Parker looking at him. He smiled back and said: "And I trust Mrs. Parker will walk out with me—halfway."

Dorothy Parker | 15

Dorothy Parker Today

On June 7, 1967, Dorothy Parker could finally put to rest her questions about the afterlife. She suffered a fatal heart attack in her apartment, with only her poodle for company. Her obituary was splashed on the front page of the *New York Times* the next day. Summing up her impact was *New Yorker* editor William Shawn's assessment that Parker's personal and literary style "were not only highly characteristic of the twenties, but also had an influence on the character of the twenties—at least that particular nonserious, insolemn sophisticated literary circle—she was an important part of New York City."

And indeed, that assessment still stands today, with only one revision: she *is* an important part of New York City. A few years after Dorothy's death, Viking Press issued an expanded edition of *The Portable Dorothy Parker*. The editors added play and book reviews and short fiction. Over the next forty years, three full-length biographies covered her life in detail. Parker's poetry, short fiction, and theater reviews were collected and printed in new editions.

Figure 5. In 1933 Dorothy Parker celebrated her fortieth birthday by meeting her second husband and preparing to leave New York for California. *Source:* Dorothy Parker Society Archives.

Of her fellow Vicious Circle members, Parker is among the few who has remained in print continuously since her lifetime. Her friends Franklin P. Adams, Robert Benchley, Heywood Broun, Laurence Stallings, Donald Ogden Stewart, and Alexander Woollcott all slowly faded as time passed and their books disappeared from shelves. Parker and Edna Ferber still top backlists, and George S. Kaufman has a play in some high school this week.

The Portable Dorothy Parker has been in bookshops since 1944, when she first compiled and arranged it. Part of the *Portable*'s attraction lies in the relevance of the observations as well as in the immediacy of the physical settings. Parker wrote about 68th Street; the brownstones on that block are still standing one hundred years later. Parker frequented the Belasco, the New Amsterdam, the Cort—all theaters that have shows running this month. Her subject matter—honeymooners, telephone conversations, cousins, parties—is just as relevant today as when Herbert Hoover was in the White House.

"A Telephone Call" (1927), one of her most popular short stories, is included in countless modern anthologies. Nearly a century after she wrote the story it was successfully presented on a tiny New York stage using a mobile phone as the lone prop—without changing a word of dialogue. Present-day visitors to the Algonquin Hotel ask the staff if they can check into Parker's old room and order her favorite cocktails to try to relive her life among her coterie of friends. Everywhere one looks today, from the dim lights in the Algonquin's lounge to the blinking marquees of the theater district, Dorothy Parker's humor and insight still ring true.

She was a woman of paradoxes: the self-described "little Jewish girl" who was educated by Catholic nuns, a caustic and often relentless social critic who was touchingly fond of animals and rarely without a pet dog, the dinner guest whom everyone wanted to be seated next to yet who was often lonely. Her exciting and sometimes tragic life bounced her all around Manhattan so that few places there escaped her keen eye and often brutally insightful pen.

Dorothy Parker has become inseparable from Gotham. Any Broadway theater open since 1920 probably had her in an aisle seat at some time. From apartments and hotels to bars and theaters, from dog-walking parks to the offices of friends and colleagues, each place she wrote about helps complete the picture. The following pages explore Dorothy Parker through the New York that she inhabited. *Dorothy Parker's New York* examines where this native New Yorker lived and worked in an effort not just to understand Dorothy better but also to get a better sense of New York City.

Each location described here affected her in some fundamental way. In some locations, the connection is direct and obvious; in others, the effect on our understanding of Dorothy is cumulative and subtle. But each place guided her career and her legacy and is thus certainly worth including on the journey.

Dorothy Parker | 17

2

An Apprenticeship in Cynicism
A Comfortable, Tumultuous Childhood

Dorothy Parker was good at laughing off her Garden State roots, joking that because her parents got her back home to Manhattan before Labor Day, she could be considered a true New Yorker. For the first twenty-three years of her life, she lived on Manhattan's Upper West Side. Like many New York City children, she spent her childhood in apartments. Dorothy was the youngest of four children, and her parents needed the space that a brownstone could provide. The neighborhood was bordered by Central Park to the East and the Hudson River to the West, though within those bounds her father never stayed in one place for more than a few years. She had lived in almost a dozen places by the time she was twenty. Most of the Rothschilds' apartments were between the West Sixties and the West Eighties, not far from Central Park, and in them Dorothy crafted her first sonnets for her father. She walked her beloved Boston terriers, Rags and Nogi, in Riverside Park and Central Park.

After briefly attending a finishing school in Morristown, New Jersey, she spent her teenage years taking care of her father and working odd jobs. Young Dorothy played the wisecracker and smart aleck from a young age—as the baby in the family, she probably developed these attributes naturally, as a defense mechanism. The precocious child would soon show exceptionally early development and maturity, especially in mental aptitude.

But she rarely wrote anything about these early years and avoided talking about them. In an interview eleven years before her death, she said, "All those writers who write about their childhood! Gentle God, if I wrote about mine you wouldn't sit in the same room with me."[1]

Until the mid-nineteenth century, most of Manhattan's residents lived on the southern end of the island, below what is today 14th Street, but as the population swelled in size during the immigration boom, the city pushed north and the Upper West Side became desirable. Many second-generation immigrants took apartments in the new neighborhoods of brownstones and apartment houses going up west of Central Park, which opened in 1859. Dorothy's parents, Henry and Eliza, though not rich were sufficiently well-off to join the upper middle class there.

Here on the West Side was where New York's first subway, August Belmont's Interborough Rapid Transit (IRT), opened when Dorothy was nine. By cutting the commuting time between downtown and the new uptown neighborhoods, the subway made possible the construction of thousands of apartments for the middle class and, for the better-off, spectacular apartment buildings such as the Dakota, the Ansonia, and the Dorilton. In the middle of it all was "the Boulevard"—today called Broadway—with landscaped trees and streetcar tracks in the median.

Seashore Birthplace and Tribute

Figure 6. The Fountain Apartments in Long Branch, New Jersey, have a literary landmark attached to a lamp post. The Rothschild summer cottage was once on this lot. *Source:* Photo by the author.

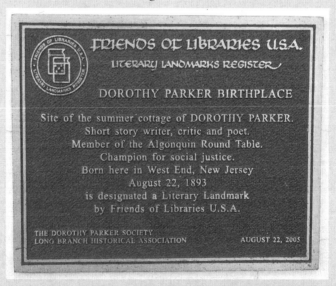

Dorothy Parker's birthplace is a sleepy little village that is part of Long Branch in Monmouth County, New Jersey. It lies just sixty miles from Manhattan; in the 1890s it was reachable from New York by steam ferry and railroad. The Rothschilds' cottage, with a separate carriage house, was near the present-day **732 Ocean Avenue**, across the street from the beach.

20 | Dorothy Parker's New York

Like the neighboring beach communities of Elberon and Deal, West End was a small town that swelled in the summer. In the nineteenth century, Long Branch was among the most desirable places for New Yorkers to spend the sweltering summers. Locals brag that seven U.S. presidents visited there, and President Ulysses S. Grant's "summer White House" is a source of pride. The streets are lined with stately Victorians that have survived into the twenty-first century, contrasting with the numerous plain-looking condominiums that have been erected more recently along the water. Unlike Newport, Rhode Island, which drew mostly WASPs, the Jersey Shore drew many upper-class Jewish families. Among these was the prominent banking family, the Seligmans, as well as members of the extended Guggenheim family, who were the Rothschilds' next-door neighbors.

Although Dorothy's birth was a happy event in West End, the village would forever be tinged with sadness for the family. A month shy of young Dottie's fifth birthday, her mother died at the house of coronary artery disease. Although it is not clear whether the Rothschilds ever returned to West End after Eliza's death, records show that the cottage burned down some years later. Henry held onto the property almost until his death.

More than a century after Dottie's birth, her birthplace was designated the first national literary landmark in the Garden State. In 2005, Friends of Libraries USA honored her with a marker in West End, a dedication cosponsored by the Dorothy Parker Society and the Long Branch Historical Association. A bronze plaque is attached to the entrance of the Fountain Apartments at 732 Ocean Avenue.

A Developing Wit

The cynicism and mordant wit that were the hallmarks of Parker's career did not appear suddenly with her first job at *Vogue*; they were the product of a tumultuous childhood. On one hand, Dorothy led a comfortable life as a young girl, summering on the Jersey Shore and at Long Island resorts, attending Broadway shows, and studying at one of the area's finest schools. However, her girlhood wasn't always pleasant: Dorothy's mother died right before she turned five, her three siblings were quite a bit older, she had an evangelical stepmother bent on saving her Jewish soul for Jesus, and she spent hours alone with books rather than playmates.

Despite having a Jewish father and Episcopalian mother, Dorothy attended a Roman Catholic convent school with her older sister, Helen. When she wasn't having run-ins with the nuns or her family, young Dorothy was reading voraciously—a practice she later claimed was much better than a formal education. She devoured William Makepeace Thackeray's Victorian classic *Vanity Fair*, no doubt identifying with the novel's plain yet dangerously seductive protagonist, Rebecca Sharpe. Parker reminisced in 1956, "I read *Vanity Fair* about a dozen times a year. I was a woman of eleven when I first read it—the thrill of that line 'George Osborne lay dead with a bullet through his heart.'"

In 1906, like almost every other girl in New York, Dorothy was crazy about the stage sensation *Peter Pan* and its star, Maude Adams, and collected her photos. She also was a devoted fan of *St. Nicholas* magazine for children, filled with poetry, stories, cartoons, and humor. Generations of American children grew up reading short fiction and poetry interspersed with cartoons from this periodical—it was almost like *The New Yorker* for the junior set.

In the end, literature provided a literal escape as well. In 1914 the twenty-one-year-old Dorothy Rothschild submitted a biting look at summer hotel conversation titled "Any Porch" to *Vanity Fair*, and it was accepted. This led to a junior staff position with the Condé Nast publishing company and enabled her to take a room at a neighborhood boardinghouse. While working for *Vogue* and *Vanity Fair*, Dorothy commuted via the new IRT. She submitted some poems to magazines and newspapers under her given name, Dorothy Rothschild, but sent others under made-up names such as "Henriette Rousseau" and "Helen Wells." She set many of her most famous stories and poems in the neighborhood she knew so well, the Upper West Side.

Figure 7. Verdi Square and Broadway as it looked when Dorothy Rothschild was a teenager. *Source:* Public Domain.

This neighborhood, dominated by block after block of large apartment houses interspersed with wonderful four- and five-story brownstones and magnificent beaux arts buildings, is essentially unchanged since Parker lived there many decades ago. In her day it was becoming a haven for the upper middle class, whose lifestyle she portrayed in much of her work. Short stories such as "The Waltz" and "The Garter" are set at parties that appear to take place in the neighborhood. Her short story "Sentiment," published in May 1933 in *Harper's Bazaar*, is set inside a taxicab hurrying down these very streets:

And then there's the doctor's house, and the three thin gray houses and then—oh, God, we must be at our house now! Our house, though we had only the top floor. And I loved the long, dark stairs, because he climbed them every evening. And our little prim pink curtains at the windows, and the boxes of geraniums that always grew for me. And the little stiff entry and the funny mail-box, and his ring at the bell. . . . I will see our tree and our house again, and then my heart will burst and I will be dead. I will look, I will look.

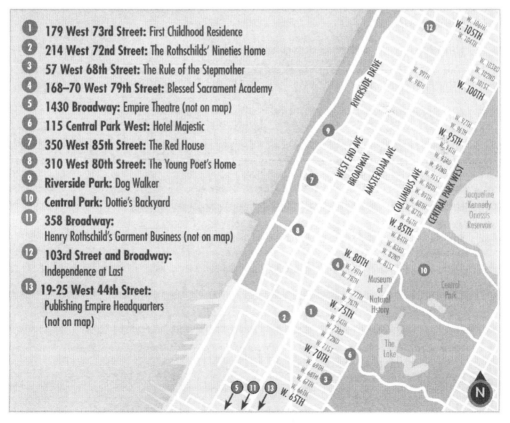

Figure 8. Map of the Upper West Side showing locations of Dorothy Parker homes and haunts. *Source:* Collection of the author.

An Apprenticeship in Cynicism | 23

Dorothy Comes Home

Henry and Eliza Rothschild weren't expecting their family's new addition to be born while they were still at their summer cottage in West End, New Jersey. Eliza, a frail woman in her forties, was seven months pregnant, and Henry thought the sea air would do her good. Years later Dorothy quipped, "That was the last time I was early for anything."

When Eliza was well enough to travel, mother and baby were brought home to [1] **179 West 73rd Street**, a few steps east of Amsterdam Avenue. The Rothschild family had lived here since at least 1892. Her father was listed as a cloak maker in the city directory. When Dorothy was a baby, this was a beautiful area of handsome brownstones with front stoops, awnings, and tree-lined streets. Overhead, one would see the wires of the New York Telephone Company, created in 1895 to serve fifteen thousand subscribers with simple four-digit numbers. Streetcars ran up the wide avenues, though horse-drawn hansom cabs were still a common sight on the streets. Although many of the other brownstones from the era have survived to this day, the Rothschilds' building was demolished for a large apartment building sometime before World War II.

The Rothschilds' Nineties Home

When Dorothy Rothschild was still an infant, her parents moved the family to [2] **214 West 72nd Street**, a few doors down from Broadway, then called simply the Boulevard.[2] All the apartments Henry bought or rented were near the 72nd Street address. At the time, rents in New York were reasonable, with new apartments being built at a rapid pace. Landlords seeking well-off, reliable tenants like the Rothschilds offered incentives to move, which likely accounted for many of the family's frequent relocations. At the time, New York still upheld the madness of "Moving Day" on May 1. From the colonial era up to World War II, all leases expired simultaneously at 9:00 a.m., which meant thousands of residents changed addresses on the same exact day.

When baby Dorothy lived in this four-story private house, the building had awnings, a garden, a front stoop, and an entranceway lined with glass. Her parents and older siblings, Harold, Bertram, and Helen, occupied several rooms. Dorothy probably lived there until her mother passed away at forty-seven, just shy of the child's fifth birthday. The handsome gray stone home was demolished in 2019 and a bland residence replaced it. The developers, who had begged the community board for permission to tear down "Dorothy Parker's Childhood Home" made an effort to keep the bad juju away by naming their uninspired building "Parker West."

The neighborhood remains one of the most desirable in all of New York, with some of the finest schools, best restaurants, and most fashionable homes. When it came time to find another apartment, Henry didn't look too far: West 68th Street was just around the corner.

Not Easy Being a Stepdaughter

At the turn of the century, Henry moved the family from West 72nd Street to a limestone row house at **[3] 57 West 68th Street**. He also remarried, to schoolteacher Eleanor Frances Lewis. The rather hasty remarriage to a Sunday school spinster didn't sit well with his children, especially his youngest daughter. Dorothy disliked this woman who

Figure 9. The third childhood home of Dorothy Rothschild was built in 1900, and the family may have been the first or second to reside here. *Source:* Photo by the author.

barged into her life when she was only six years old, resenting her role as a replacement for her mother. She hated being forced to say prayers before she went to bed and was loath to call the woman *Mother* or any similar term.

"She was crazy with religion," Dorothy confided to her friend Wyatt Cooper in the 1960s.[3] "I'd come in from school; she'd greet me with 'Did you love Jesus today?' Now, how do you answer that? She was hurt because the older ones called her 'Mrs. Rothschild.' What else? That was her name. I didn't call her anything. 'Hey, you' was about the best I could do." Maybe Dorothy was praying hard for something else; Eleanor died before the little girl turned ten.

On those rare occasions when Parker spoke of her childhood, she liked to make it appear that she had grown up in a Dickensian household. But she told at least one story that points to the loneliness of being the youngest in the family by six years. One of her brothers was walking down the street with a pal, and they passed Dorothy. When the friend asked him if she was his little sister, he casually replied no, within earshot of the child, and they kept walking without a backward glance.

The family's nondescript row house still stands between Columbus Avenue and Central Park West. On the block are the same classic brownstones, the synagogue, and the Second Church of Christ, Scientist that Dorothy would have been familiar with as a girl. The block is also the former home of James Dean, who moved to **19 West 68th Street** (a fifth-floor walkup) in the spring of 1953; Roy Schatt's iconic photo of Dean walking down a car-lined street was taken here. These days it is still a quiet residential block, much as it was when Dorothy was a young girl walking to school or to Central Park with her constant companions, her dogs.

The Nuns and the Little Jewish Girl

The **[4] Blessed Sacrament Academy at 168–70 West 79th Street**, between Amsterdam and Columbus avenues, is still standing. This is where, as a young girl, Dorothy Rothschild first honed the wit and talent that would make her famous. "Convents do the same things progressive schools do, only they don't know it," Parker told the *Paris Review* in 1956. "They don't teach you how to read; you have to find out for yourself. At my convent we did have a textbook, one that devoted a page and a half to Adelaide Anne Proctor; but we couldn't read Dickens; he was vulgar, you know."

Dorothy and big sister Helen, with a six-year age difference, were students at the academy in 1900 when Dorothy was seven. Parker told interviewers late in life that she had loathed the place and joked that the school was chosen only because she wouldn't have to cross any avenues to get there. To get her in, her father had claimed that she was Episcopalian, but Dorothy couldn't quite pull that off and often felt both isolated and

26 | Dorothy Parker's New York

Figure 10. The 1900 double brownstone building that was Dorothy Rothschild's elementary school remains an educational institution today. *Source:* Photo by the author.

out of place. By all accounts, she drove the nuns crazy. It's easy to imagine that Dorothy's technique of muttering one-liners under her breath was perfected in the halls of Blessed Sacrament. Today the double brownstone still looks much the same, and it remains a school, though not a Catholic one. In a stroke of irony that even Dorothy would enjoy, the current tenants are Rodeph Sholom School, an independent Reform Jewish day school.

A Young Fan of Peter Pan

When James M. Barrie's *Peter Pan* debuted in America at the **[4] Empire Theatre, 1430 Broadway** (between 40th and 41st), in November 1905, twelve-year-old Dorothy Rothschild was among the young girls who contributed to its instant success. She was close to her sister, Helen, so perhaps they took in the show together. Girls at the time tried to outdo one another in repeat attendances of the show, which starred Maude Adams as Peter. Sitting in the audience with crisp white handkerchiefs, they waved furiously to show that *yes*, they did believe in fairies. *Peter Pan* ran from 1905 to 1907 at the Empire with Adams, and she returned to the role there in 1912 and 1915. While on vacation in Bellport, Long Island, in June 1906, young Dorothy implored her father in a note, "If you see any pictures of Maude Adams, please send them to me."[4] This early exposure to the magic of Broadway likely gave her a taste for the critic's life; a little more than ten years later, she was back at the same theater as a reviewer. The theater was demolished in 1953; now, an office building stands at the same location.

Coming of Age in New York

The years of Dorothy's childhood travails—from the death of her stepmother through her return from boarding school and the time immediately afterward—are sketchy at best. She spent summers with her sister at resorts on Long Island, but she wrote little. More than likely, most of her time was spent in the company of her father, whose health was deteriorating. Henry moved the two of them to several different apartment houses on the Upper West Side; all the homes were near each other and the park.

Figure 11. The original Hotel Majestic as seen from Central Park, circa 1905. *Source:* Detroit Publishing Company, Library of Congress, Prints and Photographs Division.

28 | Dorothy Parker's New York

At sixteen, her schooling behind her, Dorothy was living with her now-twice-widowed father in the [6] **Hotel Majestic, 115 Central Park West**, a deluxe residential hotel overlooking Central Park. Across the street were the Dakota Apartments, famous for being the first (wildly successful) attempt to bring many wealthy families under one roof. Two blocks away was her childhood home. Below her windows spread the beautiful park, where she could walk her dogs as she tried to figure out what to do with her life.

The Majestic was a luxury hotel built in 1894 by Albert Zucker. Twelve stories tall, it had private bowling alleys, a grand lobby, horse-drawn carriages out front, and a rooftop garden. With its six hundred rooms, it was one of the best places to live in the city, and being there gave young Dorothy a chance to observe firsthand many of the well-to-do people who would later resurface in her fiction and poetry. Her story "An Apartment House Anthology," published in the *Saturday Evening Post* of August 20, 1921, could easily be set in the Majestic:

> What is really the keynote of the Tippetts' living room is the copy of the Social Register lying temptingly open on the table. It is as if Mrs. Tippett had been absorbed in it, and had only torn herself from its fascinating pages in order to welcome you. It is almost impossible for you to overlook the volume, but if you happen to, Mrs. Tippett will help you out by pointing to it with an apologetic little laugh. No one knows better than she, she says, that its orange-and-black binding is all out of touch with the color scheme of the room; but, you see, she uses it for a telephone book and she is simply lost without it. Just what Mrs. Tippett does when she wants to look up the telephone number of her laundress or her grocer is not explained.[5]

The Majestic currently at 115 Central Park West is not the same building that Dorothy resided in as a teenager. The Hotel Majestic was demolished at the end of the 1920s, and the current art deco building on the site opened in 1931. Its two towers, designed by Irwin S. Chanin and Jacques Delamarre, rise twenty-nine stories and serve as home to many wealthy residents of the city, just as the original Majestic did in Dorothy's life. In fact, Round Table members George and Beatrice Kaufman were on one floor and Edna Ferber on another at the Majestic.

A Young Poet Grows Up

During this time, the family hopped from one apartment to the next, always looking for better rents and a fresh start. They found a good deal on the West Side, only five blocks away, in an even more spectacular apartment house at [7] **350 West 85th Street**, a luxurious six-story red-brick building between West End Avenue and Riverside Drive. Named "the Red House," it was designed and built by Harde & Short in 1904 and is a city landmark today. It has a combination of French neo-Gothic and Renaissance elements. It was built at a time when apartments were replacing row houses as the Upper West Side's dominant type of residence.

The Red House, which resembles an Elizabethan manor house, is practically across the street from Riverside Park and its views of the Hudson River. It would have been a convenient spot for someone with a household of dogs, providing an easy base from which to walk them. This girlhood home of Dorothy's is almost directly across the street from the 1920s home of Heywood Broun and Ruth Hale, at 333 West 85th Street. Many legendary parties were held in the Broun-Hale home, which Heywood had won in a high-stakes poker game. (Fittingly, he later lost it at the card table.)

After leaving the Majestic, the family moved to a beautiful six-story limestone apartment house at [8] **310 West 80th Street**, between West End Avenue and Riverside Drive. Dorothy's older brothers and sister soon moved to homes of their own, however, leaving the teenager alone to care for her father. Henry was not well, suffering from the failing heart that would eventually kill him. As with Dorothy, death was also at the forefront of Henry's mind; he had already lost two wives, his younger brother, and both parents. Now it was just Henry, Dorothy, and the dogs.

Young Dorothy penned early pieces of light verse during this time. Only scraps survive, from postcards and letters sent to her father. He wrote back to her, always in sonnets and ballads. In that row house, getting older, deciding what she wanted to do with her life, she quite possibly dreamed of becoming a professional writer. In the summer of 1905, around the time she was living at this address, she sent a letter to her father from Long Island:

I am having a lot of fun,
Tho' my neck and arms
Are burned by the sun.
Doesn't "tho" look poetic?
—Dorothy

On December 27, 1913, Henry Rothschild suffered a fatal heart attack. He was buried next to his wives in Woodlawn Cemetery. His daughter would tell people she was now an orphan (despite being twenty years old). In 2009, the Dorothy Parker Society dedicated a small bronze plaque on the building exterior.

Girlhood Walk

Visitors to New York who think that the only park in Manhattan is Central Park are missing out on a special place. [9] **Riverside Park** is a narrow, 266-acre gem squeezed between the Hudson River and Riverside Drive. It was planned and laid out by Frederick Law Olmsted, the architect who cocreated Central Park. Young Dorothy Rothschild came here on family outings to the Soldiers' and Sailors' Monument, located at 89th Street and Riverside Drive. A family photo shows her holding her dogs in front of the monument.

When Dorothy was young, the monument, with its marble sculpture and graceful terraces, was brand-new. It was completed in 1902, at a time when nostalgia for the Civil War was high. The cylindrical building is an enlarged version of the Hellenistic

Figure 12. This grand Civil War memorial in Riverside Park is the focus of annual neighborhood Memorial Day ceremonies. *Source:* Photo by the author.

Monument of Lysicrates in Athens. The names of the military leaders Sherman and Farragut are inscribed there, along with such battle sites as Gettysburg, Vicksburg, and Antietam. This is a lovely, quiet place to bring a book. The twenty-minute walk from Riverside Park to Central Park is one of the most enjoyable strolls to be found in Manhattan.

Dorothy's Backyard

Except for the years she would later spend in California and Pennsylvania, Dorothy spent her entire life within a few blocks of **[10] Central Park**. But as a child, she wasn't much interested in skipping rope, and she had few friends. More likely, Dorothy found the park a peaceful place to walk her dogs, just as residents do a century later. In a city of paved streets, it is the woodsy backyard for more than 1.5 million Manhattan residents, and more than 42 million people visit it each year. When she wasn't walking her dog in the park, Dorothy likely walked with her sister. But they didn't frolic on play structures; playgrounds were not popular in Central Park in the early twentieth century, and the wealthy residents of apartment buildings bordering the park fought the city to prevent their installation. The first playgrounds in the park were built in 1934.

The Life of Reilly

Dorothy Parker's love of animals, especially dogs and horses, is well documented. She was almost never without a pet dog. In July 1921 she published "To My Dog" in *Life*. It could just as well have been written about a man as about man's best friend:

> I often wonder why on earth
> > You rate yourself so highly;
> A shameless parasite, from birth
> > You've lived the life of Reilly.
> No claims to fame distinguish you;
> > Your talents are not many;
> You're constantly unfaithful to
> > Your better self—if any.
> Yet you believe, with faith profound,
> > The world revolves around you;
> May I point out, it staggered 'round
> > For centuries without you?

Parker particularly loved strays and once rescued one late at night on Sixth Avenue. She took the pooch home, cleaned it up, and presented it to affluent friends on Long Island. The thought of a mutt living in such rich digs amused her. She had dogs as companions throughout her life, no matter where she was living. She even signed telegrams to friends and family as if from her pooch. When she sat for portraits, she liked having a dog for company. And when she passed away in 1967, she was living alone with a poodle.

Horses also frequent Dorothy's writing; she may have grown up a city girl, but horses were a big part of her daily life. After a night on the town, Dorothy was known to stop and admire hansom cabs. Her short story "Just a Little One," published by *The New Yorker* in May 1928, conveys her feelings: "Don't let me take any horses home with me. It doesn't matter so much about stray dogs and kittens, but elevator boys get awfully stuffy when you try to bring in a horse. You might just as well know that about me now, Fred. You can always tell that the crash is coming when I start getting tender about Our Dumb Friends. Three highballs, and I think I'm St. Francis of Assisi." By the end of the story, she wants to "go out and get a horsie."

The Garment Business

Henry Rothschild had a thriving men's cloak and suit business at [11] **358 Broadway**, between Franklin and Leonard streets, when daughter Dorothy was born in 1893. Her father was "a fairly prosperous cloak and suiter" employing more than two hundred workers in the booming garment industry. A merchandising pioneer in the wholesale men's suit trade, he was among the most prosperous garment industry executives of the era, doing well enough to be admitted to exclusive associations such as the Union Club. The 1893 New York City Directory lists 358 Broadway as Rothschild's business. It was probably an office or showroom, with workers in other buildings (away from the public eye) sewing the merchandise.

It is not known whether Henry Rothschild used sweatshops full of women and children to make the garments for his firm; if not, he would have been a most remarkable exception, for this practice was all but universal at the time. New York City's sweatshops have a tragic history. The 1911 Triangle Shirtwaist Factory fire, for instance, which claimed the lives of 146 workers—many of them immigrant girls—occurred at **23–29 Washington Place**, at the northern corner of Washington Square East, a little over a mile from Rothschild's store. Henry Rothschild was not completely unmindful of his workers, however. At Christmastime, he and Dorothy traveled in a horse-drawn coach to the Lower East Side, where many workers lived. She watched from the carriage while her father handed out neatly sealed envelopes of cash to those in need.

An Apprenticeship in Cynicism | 33

Figure 13. This is a similar catalogue to styles Dorothy Rothschild's father was manufacturing during the month that she was born in 1893. *Source: Journal of Fashion and Tailoring*, Library of Congress, Prints and Photographs Division.

Henry's former business was located in what is now TriBeCa (the "Triangle Below Canal Street"), one of the hottest neighborhoods in the city. The warehouses and factories of the old garment businesses have been revamped into spacious loft apartments, and with the influx of luxury building conversions have come upscale shops, restaurants, and art galleries.

Independence at Last

When Dorothy Rothschild sold her first poem, "Any Porch," in 1914 to Frank Crowninshield of *Vanity Fair*, her literary life began. After countless rejections from many publications, the acceptance of the poem gave her the confidence to march down to the

Condé Nast offices and seek a job. The gamble paid off; she was hired for ten dollars a week for light editorial work at *Vogue*, *Vanity Fair*'s sister publication.

With an entry-level publishing job secured, Dorothy took a room at a boardinghouse at **[12] 103rd Street and Broadway**, a building equidistant from her siblings' homes. After her father died in 1913, she had lived with them off and on. The IRT had recently opened a station at 103rd Street, and apartments were being built nearby. Dorothy's room cost eight dollars a week, which also included two meals a day. She was happy in the boardinghouse and made friends there, among them Thorne Smith, an advertising copywriter who would later create *Topper*, the popular comedy about mischievous ghosts. The precise location of the 103rd Street boardinghouse is lost to history; Dorothy never clearly pinned it down.

The neighborhood is noisy, and the rumble of the subway underneath the street corner is noticeable. We do know that Dorothy's room was a short walk from Riverside Park, a block to the west, and that she was surrounded by movie theaters, restaurants, and residences in a neighborhood that is not so different today.

It was while living on the Upper West Side that she married Edwin Pond Parker II, a young stock broker from Hartford. Their July 2, 1917, marriage ushered in a new era in Dorothy's life, when she went from Dorothy Rothschild, magazine writer, to Dorothy Parker, Jazz Age icon. When Private Parker departed from France, the couple was living at **240 West 104th Street**, on the corner of Broadway in an apartment building that is still standing.

From Vogue to Vanity Fair

The nondescript office building at **[13] 19–25 West 44th Street** was the home of the Condé Nast publishing empire before World War I. Condé Nast bought *Vogue* in 1909, when circulation was less than 23,000, and made Edna Woolman Chase managing editor in 1914. That same year Dorothy joined the staff, and she continued to work at Condé Nast until 1920—a period of remarkable growth under Chase's leadership.

Dorothy started off composing captions for fashion spreads in *Vogue*, doing the work of what today would be called an editorial assistant. Even at this early stage of her career, we see signs of the wit that was developing under her editor's nose. Among her captions were such dollops as "Brevity is the soul of lingerie—as the Petticoat said to the Chemise;" "This little pink dress will win you a beau;" and "Right Dress! For milady's motor jaunt."[6] Dorothy was the staff guinea pig for hairstyle experiments and other fashion tests. The atmosphere was fairly Victorian, and female staffers were decorous; they even wore gloves in the office.

She also sent her work across the hallway to *Vanity Fair*, which published her poetry and prose. "The Picture Gallery" appeared in the December 1918 issue under the heading "Oh, Look—I Can Do It, Too."

My life is like a picture gallery,
With narrow aisles wherein the spectators may walk.
The pictures themselves are hung to the best advantage;
So that the good ones draw immediate attention.
Now and then, one is so cleverly hung,
That, though it seems obtrusive,
It catches the most flattering light.
Even the daubs are shown so skillfully
That the shadows soften them into beauty.
My life is like a picture gallery,
With a few pictures turned discreetly to the wall.

After a few years, Dorothy tired of the white gloves and the daily office drudgery at *Vogue*. To her rescue came the "gentle and courtly" Frank Crowninshield, who made her an offer. She jumped at the opportunity to go over to *Vanity Fair*, which he had launched in 1913 for sophisticated readers. The girl who never made it past eighth grade was made a copyeditor. When critic and "Jeeves" creator P. G. Wodehouse left the magazine in 1918 to focus on his writing career, Crowninshield took a chance and assigned the office wisecracker to replace him as drama critic. She was observant, clever, and fearless—perfect characteristics for the city's first female theater critic.

The highlight of Dorothy's tenure at Condé Nast came in 1919. That year humorist Robert Benchley was hired as managing editor, and World War I combat veteran Robert E. Sherwood was brought on as a writer. The trio hit it off immediately and had a grand time as office mates. Parker stood about four feet eleven inches, Benchley six feet, and Sherwood six feet seven inches. Parker remarked about the head-turning impression the trio made together on sidewalks, saying that the little people from the Hippodrome's vaudeville shows were attracted to Sherwood for his extreme height.

Working for Condé Nast set Parker up for the professional life she chose as a writer. It was here that she got her feet wet in the publishing world and made contacts with people she would be associated with for the rest of her life. Her office was just a two-minute walk from the Algonquin Hotel, no doubt contributing to the frequency of her lunches there. As the next chapter of Parker's life began, she was headed on a new journey of success.

36 | Dorothy Parker's New York

3

Drink and Dance and Laugh and Lie
The Vicious Circle Era

After marrying Edwin Pond Parker II on July 2, 1917, Dorothy Rothschild became Dorothy Parker, the name she used for the rest of her life. She had changed professionally, too. Her informal apprenticeship was over when Frank Crowninshield tapped her to fill P. G. Wodehouse's shoes as drama critic for *Vanity Fair*, making her New York City's first female drama critic—and certainly one of its most famous.

Her professional and social lives began to blend when she took on another role that would make her a household name: reigning wit of the Algonquin Round Table. This group, an eclectic collection of columnists, publicists, playwrights, writers, and sundry friends, exchanged clever banter and social pronouncements over lunch each day at the Algonquin Hotel, located on Club Row, West 44th Street, between Fifth and Sixth avenues.

Although the group is justly famous for its wisecracking luncheons, the friendships and alliances were solidified during evening rounds at the theater, various speakeasies, and weekend lawn parties on Long Island. Indeed, members of the Round Table supported one another professionally. For Dorothy, it was the perfect stage on which to hone her craft; surrounded by brutally quick wits, she knew she had to be quicker.

Among the Round Table group of thirty was the man who would be her dear friend and mentor, Franklin P. Adams. He was the dean of the gathered friends, and at thirty-eight, the oldest. As conductor of "The Conning Tower" in the *Tribune*—and later, the *World*—he accepted contributions to his column, which was wildly popular with the

Figure 14. After launching his career in his hometown of Chicago, Franklin P. Adams became the most talked-about newspaper columnist in New York. *Source:* Franklin P. Adams Archives.

general public. Parker could be counted on to send him some of her best material. FPA did not pay writers; they submitted for the thrill and pride of being accepted. On the morning of August 16, 1925, readers of the *World* opened their newspapers to find not one, but six Parker poems. Under the heading "Some Beautiful Letters" appeared some of the most famous lines Dorothy would create in her entire career:

Observation

If I don't drive around the park,
I'm pretty sure to make my mark.
If I'm in bed each night by ten,
I may get back my looks again,
If I abstain from fun and such,
I'll probably amount to much,
But I shall stay the way I am,
Because I do not give a damn.

Social Note

Lady, lady, should you meet
One whose ways are all discreet,
One who murmurs that his wife
Is the lodestar of his life,
One who keeps assuring you
That he never was untrue,
Never loved another one . . .
Lady, lady, better run!

News Item

Men seldom make passes
At girls who wear glasses

Interview

The ladies men admire, I've heard,
Would shudder at a wicked word.
Their candle gives a single light;
They'd rather stay at home at night.
They do not keep awake till three,
Nor read erotic poetry.
They never sanction the impure,
Nor recognize an overture.
They shrink from powders and from paints . . .
So far, I've had no complaints.

Comment

Oh, life is a glorious cycle of song,
A medley of extemporanea;
And love is a thing that can never go wrong;
And I am Marie of Roumania.

Résumé

Razors pain you;
Rivers are damp;
Acids stain you;

And drugs cause cramp.
Guns aren't lawful;
Nooses give;
Gas smells awful;
You might as well live.

Wonderful Nonsense Ends

Less than ten years after the Round Table began, it silently faded into memory when the regulars suddenly found themselves taken up with new occupations and successes. Dorothy was not even there to witness the end of the era. When the twenties ended with a crash and the Algonquin hosted its last Round Table lunch, she was in Europe on an extended journey, the guest of her friends Sara and Gerald Murphy as they nursed their young son through tuberculosis.

Robert Benchley

Figure 15. Writer Robert Benchley transitioned from writer to actor, ultimately leading to a career onstage, on radio, and in film. *Source:* Dorothy Parker Society Archives.

The bonds of friendship between Dorothy Parker and Robert Benchley were exceptionally strong. They met when he was hired as managing editor of *Vanity Fair* in 1919 and she was the magazine's drama critic. They were part of the Algonquin Round Table together and collaborated on various projects with their friends. Benchley owned a home in Westchester County with his wife, Gertrude, but kept a city place. For many years, Benchley resided in the **Royalton Hotel, 44 West 44th Street**. Benchley and Parker were always very formal with one another. In 1920, "Mr. Benchley" and "Mrs. Parker" rented an office at the Metropolitan Opera House building. The space was quite small, and friends would drop by their little room for visits. Dorothy suggested they stencil on their door "The Utica Drop Forge Tool & Die Works." The building, located on 39th Street and Broadway, was built in 1883 and demolished in 1966. When Benchley made the switch from editor to performer, they spent time together in Los Angeles. His early death from alcohol abuse in 1945 affected her deeply.

The Round Table, as well as the relentless, never-ending party of the twenties, proved to be a boon for Dorothy Parker as a writer: In six years, she brought out three collections of poetry; published short fiction in such prestigious magazines as *The New Yorker*, *Vanity Fair*, *Harper's*, and *The Bookman*; won the O. Henry Award for her short story "Big Blonde;" and collaborated on several theater works, including two revues put on by members of what came to be known as the Vicious Circle.

Unfortunately, Dorothy's personal life during this period was less triumphant. She suffered the collapse of one marriage, a string of bad relationships and worse breakups, an abortion, hospitalization for nervous exhaustion, and at least three suicide attempts.

Always Someone on Her Arm

After her marriage to Eddie fell apart in the early 1920s, Dorothy was not at a loss for lovers. Although often lonely even in the company of friends, she—much like her character Hazel Morse in "Big Blonde"—managed to find willing male companions in an extended circle of friends and acquaintances. She counted among her many boyfriends Seward Collins, her editor at *The Bookman*, who ditched her when he tired of her by taking extended trips to Palm Beach; and Charles MacArthur, a newspaperman, raconteur, and budding playwright who was also Robert Benchley's drinking buddy. Parker was madly in love with Charlie. Unfortunately, Charlie had other lovers as well as a wife back home in Chicago, and the affair ended miserably with an abortion and Parker's attempted suicide.

Nor did Parker's choice of boyfriends improve with time. In 1931 she met John McClain, a clerk in a Wall Street brokerage house. He was a good-looking rake of twenty-seven who had played football for Brown, and Mrs. Parker, thirty-eight, liked the attention he gave her. They soon became an item. Both got what they wanted: She, fearful that her youth and popularity were declining precipitously, acquired a handsome boyfriend; he acquired attention from the press merely by virtue of being the man on her arm. He also acquired a better career. Parker spoke to a friend at the *New York Sun*, who found a reporter's job for McClain. Parker craved McClain's attention. When he wasn't visiting her room at the Algonquin, she would telephone him throughout the day and night. He was less enamored and, by most accounts, after using her to get in the society pages, tossed her aside. Parker responded with a suicide attempt.

Aging Disgracefully

As she hit her thirties, Dorothy found herself moving from one lover to another, seemingly unable—or perhaps unwilling—to build a stable relationship, constantly seeking new conquests to keep herself entertained. In a candid moment of self-awareness and premonition in June 1924, she penned this ballad:

Ballade at Thirty-Five

This, no song of an ingénue,
    This, no ballad of innocence;
This, the rhyme of a lady who
    Followed ever her natural bents.
    This, a solo of sapience,
This, a chantey of sophistry,
    This, the sum of experiments,
I loved them until they loved me.

Decked in garments of sable hue,
    Daubed with ashes of myriad Lents,
Wearing shower bouquets of rue,
        Walk I ever in penitence.
        Oft I roam, as my heart repents,
Through God's acre of memory,
    Marking stones, in my reverence,
"I loved them until they loved me."

Pictures pass me in long review,
  Marching columns of dead events.
I was tender and, often, true;
  Ever a prey to coincidence.
  Always knew I the consequence;
Always saw what the end would be.
  We're as Nature has made us, hence
I loved them until they loved me.

L'ENVOI

Princes, never I'd give offense,
  Won't you think of me tenderly?
Here's my strength and my weakness, gents,
  I loved them until they loved me.

Reign of the Round Table

Hotels make unusual locations for literary history, and hotels in New York with true artistic connections are scarce. The Shelton (now student housing) was home to Georgia O'Keeffe and Alfred Stieglitz for a decade. Media tycoon William Randolph Hearst built the Warwick for his famous friends. The Plaza is home to fictional six-year-old Eloise. The Waldorf-Astoria welcomed residents Arthur Miller, Marilyn Monroe, and Cole Porter. And the Chelsea was the domicile of Sherwood Anderson, Brendan Behan, William S. Burroughs, Thomas Wolfe, and scores more. But none still draw writers today like the 1902 red-brick gem on the edge of the Theater District.

[1] **The Algonquin Hotel**, at **59 West 44th Street**, is a literary landmark for another reason: it was a destination for writers and their de facto clubhouse. When a group of rascals made it their lunch spot for a decade, it achieved fame on a whole new level as the locus of the city's first literary celebrity group. Among the group welcoming Aleck Woollcott back home from the Great War one day in June 1919 were Heywood Broun, age thirty, a newspaper writer who could cover the Giants-Cubs game at noon and an Ethel Barrymore opening in the evening, and newspaper critic George S. Kaufman, age thirty, who had one play (a flop) to his credit. Dorothy, age twenty-five, was then the drama critic at *Vanity Fair*.

While a sergeant on the U.S. Army newspaper *Stars and Stripes*, Woollcott had befriended a roster of New Yorkers who were also in publishing. The paper's editor was journeyman reporter Harold Ross, the only private in Paris with his own business cards. Franklin P. Adams, New York's most popular columnist, was a captain on the staff.

Drink and Dance and Laugh and Lie | 43

Figure 16. Map of Midtown Manhattan and the Theater District showing Algonquin Round Table hangouts. *Source:* Collection of the author.

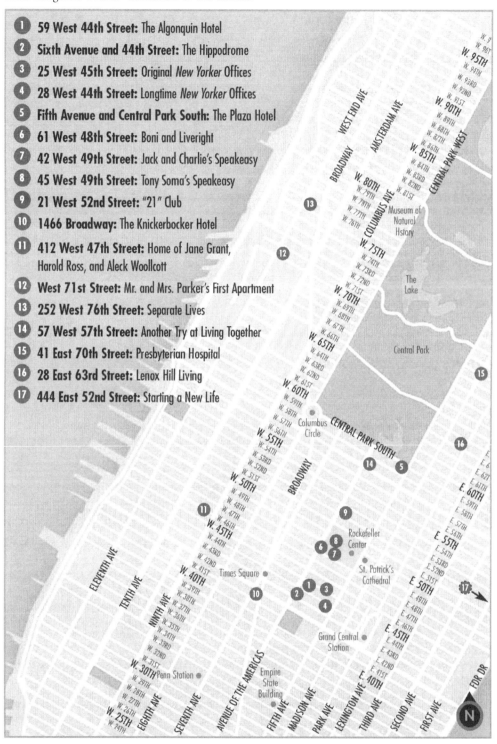

① 59 West 44th Street: The Algonquin Hotel
② Sixth Avenue and 44th Street: The Hippodrome
③ 25 West 45th Street: Original *New Yorker* Offices
④ 28 West 44th Street: Longtime *New Yorker* Offices
⑤ Fifth Avenue and Central Park South: The Plaza Hotel
⑥ 61 West 48th Street: Boni and Liveright
⑦ 42 West 49th Street: Jack and Charlie's Speakeasy
⑧ 45 West 49th Street: Tony Soma's Speakeasy
⑨ 21 West 52nd Street: "21" Club
⑩ 1466 Broadway: The Knickerbocker Hotel
⑪ 412 West 47th Street: Home of Jane Grant, Harold Ross, and Aleck Woollcott
⑫ West 71st Street: Mr. and Mrs. Parker's First Apartment
⑬ 252 West 76th Street: Separate Lives
⑭ 57 West 57th Street: Another Try at Living Together
⑮ 41 East 70th Street: Presbyterian Hospital
⑯ 28 East 63rd Street: Lenox Hill Living
⑰ 444 East 52nd Street: Starting a New Life

Other future Vicious Circle members in Paris during the war were reporters Broun and Jane Grant, and artist Neysa McMein. Serving in World War I in uniform and then seated in the Algonquin were veterans Herman J. Mankiewicz, Art Samuels, Robert E. Sherwood, Laurence Stallings (awarded the Purple Heart and Croix de Guerre), Donald Ogden Stewart, David H. Wallace, and John V. A. Weaver.

Many of the Round Table members, including Adams and Broun, were among the most popular journalists of their era. Their fans devoured their pronouncements and quoted their judgments as gospel. Yet today they are virtually forgotten. Though they wrote enough to fill a bookshelf of volumes, nothing they penned has been in print for decades. But in Parker's time, they were stars. Of the other Round Table members, only Robert Benchley, Harpo Marx, Robert E. Sherwood, Edna Ferber, and George S. Kaufman still shine, and that is probably because they were connected to the stage and screen and not just the printed page.

Parker was one of the few female members of the Vicious Circle. Jane Grant, the first woman to become a general assignment reporter at the *Times*, was married to Harold

Figure 17. The Algonquin Hotel, where a room with a bathroom cost $2 to $3 a day, opened in 1902. When the Round Table started meeting in June 1919, the hotel had already been home to many writers and Broadway stars, such as Lady Gregory, John Drew, and Ethel Barrymore. *Source:* Photo by the author.

Ross; Ruth Hale, a Broadway press agent, was married to Broun; and editor Beatrice Kaufman would drop in on her husband, George. On Saturday afternoons, Ferber would take a break from her typewriter and McMein would put down her paintbrushes to join the group in the Rose Room. Other members were fascinating women: Margaret Leech was a Vassar grad and magazine writer who went on to win two Pulitzer Prizes in history. Peggy Wood and Margalo Gillmore were native New Yorkers who starred on Broadway; their careers stretched into films and live television. It is Dorothy who is remembered most for being a part of the group, and it is the things she said at the table that are the most famous. At the top was her response when an acquaintance informed Dorothy that President Calvin Coolidge had died: "How can they tell?" As her reputation grew, Kaufman sagely predicted that everything funny he ever said would someday be attributed to her.

Stuart Y. Silverstein, who edited *Not Much Fun: The Lost Poems of Dorothy Parker*, said that the legacy of the Round Table is timeless: "The term 'the Algonquin Round Table' still holds substantial cultural resonance; for example, during [a recent] television season, at least three sitcoms employed it as an ironic punch line to skewer characters who spoke badly or stupidly. Is there any other person, or institution, or event from the interwar period that could possibly be used by a mass-market medium as an implicitly understood cultural reference? I cannot think of any—not even Lindbergh, not anymore. Perhaps the stock market crash. Endurance is its own testament."[1]

The Algonquin Hotel, the home base for the group that ruled the New York literary landscape during Prohibition, is on the edge of the theater district. Friends would meet in the Rose Room for long, uproarious lunches. Some nights there would be a poker game upstairs. After Dorothy split from Eddie for a second time in 1924, she moved into a furnished second-floor suite at the Algonquin. Dorothy returned again in 1932; this is where she made one of her suicide attempts, this time with sleeping pills. Legend has it that she tossed a drinking glass out the window to draw attention to her plight.

Even when she wasn't depressed, Dorothy wasn't exactly a good tenant, and management couldn't count on her to pay the bill. Around Christmas one year, a friend asked Dorothy if she was going to hang up a holiday stocking in her room. "No, I'm going to hang up [manager] Frank Case instead" was the ready reply.

"The Gonk," designed by Goldwin Starrett, opened for business in 1902. It is on the same street as the historic New York Yacht Club (37 West 44th), the Harvard Club (27 West 44th), the Penn Club (30 West 44th), the Bar Association (42 West 44th), and, on the other side of Fifth Avenue, the Cornell Club (6 East 44th)—hence, the street's nickname "Club Row." But even before the Round Table gang showed up, the

46 | Dorothy Parker's New York

place had a literary past; H. L. Mencken had been a guest years before, attracted to the Algonquin's reputation as "the most comfortable hotel in America."

After the Round Table moved on, the Algonquin continued to attract actors and literati—Douglas Fairbanks and Mary Pickford, Graham Greene, and William Saroyan all called the Gonk their home away from home, and William Faulkner drafted his Nobel Prize acceptance speech in his suite there in 1950.

The hotel was owned and managed for almost fifty years by the consummate hotelier Frank Case. "The Algonquin Hotel . . . is not the whole of New York," Case wrote in his 1938 memoir, *Tales of a Wayward Inn*. "There are other spots of interest and some distinction. The Algonquin is only the heart from which goes out warmth and light sufficient to make these other places possible for human habitation."

Case was quick to recognize the potential in currying favor with so many famous writers and wits, and his customers repaid him with generous amounts of ink in the city's daily newspapers. It was Case's custom to offer popovers to the group; the free food kept them coming back. FPA was the first to mention the Round Table, in his "Conning Tower" column; Silverstein says it is the first printed mention he can find of the group's formation. After Case's death in 1946, the Algonquin changed hands several times. In the last forty years, more than $75 million has been invested toward renovations and improvements to the Algonquin Hotel by a succession of owners and management companies. The most impressive renovation occurred in 2012, when Cornerstone Real Estate Advisers shut the hotel down completely for five months. The owners replaced 110-year-old plumbing, refurbished every room, and brought the building into the twenty-first century. During the COVID-19 pandemic, the Algonquin closed down for months. Ownership used the time to relocate the Blue Bar into the lobby and renovate the first floor.

New York's Largest Playhouse

Dorothy Parker and her Vicious Circle pals lived and worked in the shadow of the massive **[2] Hippodrome Theatre** across 44th Street from the Algonquin Hotel. Advertised as the largest theater in New York, it could seat an audience of 5,200 (for comparison, the Winter Garden, home to *Cats* for twenty-two years, seats 1,500).

The Hippodrome opened on April 12, 1905, straddling the entire east side of Sixth Avenue between 43rd and 44th streets. It was built by the same men who developed Coney Island's Luna Park, and tickets ranged in price from twenty-five cents to a dollar (about $36 today). By far the largest Broadway theater, it presented spectacular shows,

Drink and Dance and Laugh and Lie | 47

Figure 18. The Hippodrome was the brainchild of Frederic Thompson, who also cocreated Luna Park in Coney Island. *Source:* George Grantham Bain Collection, Library of Congress, Prints and Photographs Collection.

vaudeville, and silent movies. The Shuberts brought in a band of Sioux, put them in war paint, and had them perform a ghost dance in 1906. The Hippodrome could hold a two-ring circus; one memorable show featured an 8,000-gallon glass water tank that held chorus girls dressed as fish. In 1918, illusionist Harry Houdini made a five-ton elephant named Jenny and her trainer disappear on the Hippodrome stage. The publicists for the theater during the twenties were Murdock Pemberton and John Peter Toohey, original members of the Round Table.

Both the Sixth Avenue elevated train and the theater were demolished in 1939. After the building was torn down, the site became a parking lot until 1952, when a garage and office building went up at 1120 Sixth Avenue. Today, the office tower retains its Hippodrome name. Inside the office tower lobby is a jumbo-size image of the old theater, the only memento of the original building.

Prohibition in New York: The Failure of the Grand Experiment

Figure 19. Authorities dumping out illegal beer during the Prohibition Era. *Source:* Public Domain.

During World War I Congress bowed to pressure from temperance groups to turn the nation dry. The Eighteenth Amendment, which prohibited the manufacture, sale, or transportation of alcoholic beverages in the United States, was a disastrous failure. During the thirteen years Prohibition was in place, it was widely ignored. Dorothy Parker and her friends were among those who considered the law a nuisance and continued with their libertine lifestyle uninterrupted. Dottie's friend Jane Grant, a reporter for the *New York Times* and the wife of *New Yorker* editor Harold Ross, had her own personal bootlegger to supply their home with booze. Parker herself was once caught in a speakeasy raid by federal agents. Polly Adler, the city's best-known brothel owner, declared, "They might as well try to dry up the Atlantic with a post office blotter."

The Volstead Act, more formally known as the National Prohibition Enforcement Act, passed over President Woodrow Wilson's veto on October 28, 1919. The act specified the provisions of the Eighteenth Amendment, delineated fines and prison terms for violation of the law, and empowered the Bureau of Internal Revenue to enforce Prohibition.

National Prohibition went into effect at midnight on January 16, 1920. At that time Colonel Jacob Ruppert, the beer baron and owner of the New York Yankees, had increased the capacity of his brewery to 1.3 million barrels per year, up from 350,000 thirty years before. His business was closed until 1933. City bars, saloons, restaurants, and hotels were forced to stop selling alcohol—but not before hosting raucous parties. Some bartenders dressed as pallbearers; saloons brought in coffins. For thirteen years, drinking bootleg beer and distilled spirits was the norm. Wine and beer were brewed in homes, gin was made in bathtub stills, and illegal imports were brought in from Canada and Florida by rumrunners. In New York City, the number of places where liquor could be purchased more than doubled, from 15,000 legal spots to 32,000 illegal ones.

Figure 20. Looking west down 49th Street in the 1920s; all of these buildings were demolished to make way for Rockefeller Center. Dozens of them contained speakeasies. *Source: Public Domain.*

In 1924 New York City gave up trying to enforce the Volstead Act and asked the feds to step in and stop the illicit business in bootleg booze. Crime associated with speakeasies and bootlegging was rampant. Beatings, shootings, and stabbings were splashed across the newspapers. Prohibition provided a new way for city criminals to make a living; it also helped the Mafia cement its place in the underworld.

The notorious gambler Arnold Rothstein started a trucking company as a cover for his bootlegging racket. He hired gangsters such as Meyer Lansky and Benjamin Hyman "Bugsy" Siegel to run his operation to supply the city with liquor day and night. Rothstein, who lived at the **Ansonia Hotel, 2108 Broadway**, was the man who fixed the 1919 World Series between the Cincinnati Reds and the Chicago White Sox. In 1924, nineteen-year-old Joseph Bonanno worked for underworld bootleggers in Brooklyn and rose to head his own bloody Mafia family. In Queens, Vito Genovese used bread-company trucks to move alcohol around the city at night. In 1926, Congressman Fiorello La Guardia said it would take 250,000 police officers to enforce the law, and another 200,000 to keep the cops honest.

Calls for repeal of the Eighteenth Amendment began as early as 1923. A three-year investigation ordered by President Herbert Hoover confirmed in 1931 that the amendment was not being enforced in most states. In 1932 Democrats supported its repeal. The overwhelming Democratic victory encouraged Congress to pass the Twenty-First Amendment, repealing the Eighteenth on February 20, 1933. On March 22, the Volstead Act was amended to permit the sale of 3.2 percent beer and wine. Once the Twenty-First Amendment was ratified the following December, the Volstead Act became void. An estimated 1.4 billion gallons of illegal hard liquor was sold over the thirteen years Prohibition was in effect.

Beyond the Round Table

Like the transcendentalists group of the nineteenth century, the Round Table spawned a number of projects and collaborations among its members. Some of these projects, such as the musical revue *No Sirree!* were undertaken with the full support of the Round Table. Other schemes, such as Jane Grant and Harold Ross's idea to start a magazine geared toward well-to-do Manhattanites, did not garner the same support. In fact, when Ross pitched the idea to his Vicious Circle friends, few had much faith in its success, and some even told Ross to his face that he'd fail. Nevertheless, he did manage to convince a few people to go along with his plan. Grant pushed her husband to hit up a poker-playing millionaire, Raoul Fleischmann, heir to his family's baking fortune. Fleischmann kicked in $25,000 in seed money to launch *The New Yorker*, with Ross and Grant putting up the rest.

Although much of the initial work of creating the magazine was done in Ross and Grant's house in Hell's Kitchen, *The New Yorker's* official offices were located at **[3] 25 West 45th Street** from 1925 to 1935. Dorothy Parker was among the "editorial board" of Vicious Circle members whom Ross told potential advertisers and investors he had

Figure 21. Office space was leased here starting in 1925 to launch *The New Yorker*. The first decade of the magazine was published here. *Source:* Photo by the author.

lined up to work on the magazine; others included Broun, Connelly, Ferber, Kaufman, Woollcott, art director Rea Irvin, and playwright Laurence Stallings. Years later, Ross admitted to feeling sheepish about the deception; though he used their names, he never expected much—if any—work from them.

The first issue of *The New Yorker* appeared on February 21, 1925. The magazine was not a big hit with the Round Table or the target audience and almost went under a few times. In the fierce New York magazine market, the new publication had to find its voice. One of Ross's early policies was to not use bylines for contributors, which protected some of his more famous friends from catching heat from their editors for doing work for the upstart magazine. In addition, Ross couldn't pay well, so he doled out stock—worthless at the time but worth quite a bit later (Parker kept sixty-five shares until her death). In five years, the circulation climbed to 101,746; ten years after launching, it was 127,450. Today it is north of 1.2 million.

Dorothy wrote drama reviews for the first two issues and contributed poems—"Cassandra Drops into Verse" (February 28, 1925) and "Epitaph" (July 18, 1925)—at the height of her career. Parker's first *New Yorker* short story was a peek inside a speakeasy similar to Tony's. The nine-hundred-word "Dialogue at Three in the Morning" appeared in the February 13, 1926, issue: "'Plain water in mine,' said the woman in the petunia-colored hat. 'Or never mind about the water. Hell with it. Just straight Scotch. What I care? Just straight. That's me. Never gave anybody any trouble in my life. All right, they can say what they like about me, but I know—I know—I never gave anybody any trouble in my life. You can tell them that from me, see? What I care?'"

For the next five years *The New Yorker* was Dorothy's prime spot to place short fiction, and the pieces from this time are some of her best-known today, including "Arrangement in Black and White" (1927), "Just a Little One" (1928), and "You Were Perfectly Fine" (1929).

These stories helped define what would become a "*New Yorker* story": a few thousand words in length, urbane, clever, and keenly insightful. Although the magazine can boast contributors as diverse as Truman Capote, Vladimir Nabokov, E. Annie Proulx, and J. D. Salinger, a line can be traced from Parker's short fiction about Manhattan to later stories by John Cheever (more than one hundred stories) and John O'Hara (247 pieces, the magazine record).

These stories have helped the magazine define New York in the minds of readers across the country. Parker, in particular, used her status as a New Yorker both as a badge of honor and to prove a humorous point. For example, in her short story "Soldiers of the Republic" (which may not have been fiction), she relates the story of a passerby in war-torn Valencia chuckling at the funny American woman walking down the street in a big hat: "I lived in a state of puzzled pain as to why everybody on the streets laughed at me. It was not because 'West End Avenue' was writ across my face as if left there by a customs officer's chalked scrawl."[2] One famous anecdote about Dorothy's early *New Yorker* stint is often repeated. Ross spotted her in a speakeasy in the middle of the day. When he asked her why she wasn't at the office, working on a promised piece, she replied, "Someone else was using the pencil."

The New Yorker operated at that building until it moved a block away to **[4] 28 West 44th Street**, an address it would keep for nearly sixty years. Fleischmann and Ross moved the magazine there in 1935, ten years after founding it. Although life was becoming more fast-paced and "modern," Ross stipulated in the building lease that the landlord must keep at least one attendant-operated elevator in service.

Drink and Dance and Laugh and Lie | 53

Dorothy's contributions to the magazine after 1935 dropped steeply. Ross, who stayed at the helm until his early death in 1951, wanted only "funny" pieces from her, and she was tired of such writing. As she became more politically active, Parker turned away from writing fiction set in speakeasies and poems about unrequited love. After 1935 she wrote only thirteen more stories for publication, six of which appeared in *The New Yorker* (compared to twenty published from 1925 to1935 for *The New Yorker* alone). These later works included "Soldiers of the Republic" (1938), which she wrote after witnessing the civil war in Spain with her second husband, Alan Campbell.

Also working for *The New Yorker* in this building were Pauline Kael, E. J. Kahn, Joseph Mitchell, James Thurber, E. B. White, Katharine Sergeant White, and an office boy named Truman Capote. After Ross died, the editor's position fell to the taciturn William Shawn. He accepted Dorothy's last three short stories for the magazine at this office: "I Live on Your Visits" (1955), "Lolita" (1955), and "The Banquet of Crow" (1957). A plaque on the building's exterior salutes longtime *New Yorker* contributors but doesn't mention Dorothy Parker.

In 1985 publisher S. I. Newhouse Jr. bought control of *The New Yorker* for $168 million and added it to the roster of Condé Nast Publications. Newhouse instituted sweeping changes, and the staff moved out to join the company's other titles. Today, *The New Yorker* is headquartered in the Financial District.

Pink Slip in the Palm Court

The Plaza, at **Fifth Avenue and Central Park South [5]**, is a New York landmark with a distinct place in city history as the grandest hotel facing Central Park. It is also where Dorothy Parker was treated to a lovely Sunday brunch and then fired from *Vanity Fair*.[3] Dorothy was the magazine's caustic theater critic, known for her habit of skewering shows. At that time, Florenz Ziegfeld was among the most powerful men on Broadway and a frequent advertiser in Condé Nast magazines, as well as a personal friend of Nast. The trouble started when Dorothy panned one of Ziegfeld's shows, *Caesar's Wife*, comparing its star, Billie Burke, to the infamously tawdry vaudeville performer Eva Tanguay. Burke also happened to be Ziegfeld's wife.

On a Sunday in late January 1920, editor Frank Crowninshield took Dorothy to the Palm Court tearoom at the Plaza, praised her writing, and told her she'd be famous someday. Then he fired her.

Crowninshield had been instrumental in Dorothy's career growth. He had purchased her first poem and, when she was still wet behind the ears and without any magazine experience, had given her a job at *Vogue*. In six years under Crowninshield's watch, she

54 | Dorothy Parker's New York

Figure 22. A young Dorothy Parker around 1919, her last year as *Vanity Fair* drama critic. *Source:* Dorothy Parker Society Archives.

had gone from caption writer to drama critic. Now, on a snowy Sunday afternoon just days into the new decade, Dorothy was unemployed. For the rest of her life she would consider herself "freelance" and would never take a staff magazine job again.

The event at the Plaza had another lasting impact on her life. The day after Dorothy's dismissal from *Vanity Fair*, her close friends Robert Benchley, the magazine's managing editor, and critic Robert E. Sherwood, resigned in protest. The *Times* reported the news and so did FPA shortly afterward for the *World*: "R. Benchley tells me he hath resigned his position with *Vanity Fair* because they had discharged Dorothy Parker; which I am sorry for."

Dorothy may have seen it as bad timing—the same week, the thirteen-year experiment of Prohibition went into effect. To her credit, though, she harbored no ill will toward the Plaza and returned as a guest on more than one occasion, although her contemporaries noted that she could rarely afford the bill. She would simply show up at the hotel, and somehow the bill would get paid.

Since its 1907 opening, the nineteen-story beaux arts building has become a fixture in New York lore. The Beatles stayed there in 1964 while in town for the *Ed Sullivan Show*, and author Kay Thompson's famous children's books about the precocious Eloise are set there. More than forty movies have been filmed at the hotel, from *Plaza Suite* and Alfred Hitchcock's *North by Northwest* to *Arthur*. Ernest Hemingway suggested that Scott Fitzgerald (who once jumped into the fountain outside the hotel with Zelda) donate his liver to Princeton and his heart to the Plaza.

Drink and Dance and Laugh and Lie

The Plaza was the first New York hotel to be placed on the National Register of Historic Places. In 2004, it was purchased by developers and closed for four years. The majority of the hotel was converted into luxury units—some buyers spent $50 million each, and one went for $66 million—and a small fraction of the rooms (not facing Central Park) were eventually reopened to the public. In 2011, the legendary Oak Room and Oak Bar were closed.

Dorothy's First Book

By 1926, Dorothy Parker was hard up for money. Despite steady work and the dozens of articles and poems she had produced, she was not making ends meet. A Round Table connection came to her rescue: Horace Liveright, publisher at **[6] Boni & Liveright, 61 West 48th Street**. He convinced Dorothy to collect her work. Legend has it that she wanted money for a vacation to Europe, and a book would cover the costs of the ship passage. Dorothy pulled together some of her favorite pieces from the past ten years and handed them over to Liveright.

The poem that opens the collection, "Threnody," is a classic Parker piece—the narrator finds not just solace but also a social advantage in the heartbreak of a failed relationship. However, her final line twists the poem, and we are again left wondering just how serious she was.

Threnody

Lilacs blossom just as sweet
Now my heart is shattered.
If I bowled it down the street,
Who's to say it mattered?
If there's one that rode away
What would I be missing?
Lips that taste of tears, they say,
Are the best for kissing.

Eyes that watch the morning star
Seem a little brighter;
Arms held out to darkness are
Usually whiter.
Shall I bar the strolling guest,
Bind my brow with willow,

When, they say, the empty breast
Is the softer pillow?

That a heart falls tinkling down,
Never think it ceases.
Every likely lad in town
Gathers up the pieces.
If there's one gone whistling by
Would I let it grieve me?
Let him wonder if I lie;
Let him half believe me.[4]

Enough Rope (1926) was a bestseller and a smash critical success. The reception was outstanding, the reviews were good, and the royalties stunned Dorothy. She followed it up with *Sunset Gun* (1928), also for Boni and Liveright. Boni & Liveright was a 1920s publishing sensation. Among its authors was Ernest Hemingway, whose *In Our Time* it brought out in 1925, as well as Hart Crane, e. e. cummings, Theodore Dreiser, and William Faulkner. The house also published T. S. Eliot's *The Waste Land*. In 1917 Boni & Liveright began publishing the Modern Library—classic works of literature in the public domain in affordable hardcover editions. The series was extremely profitable, yet the company was in financial trouble.

When a Liveright employee, twenty-seven-year-old Bennett Cerf, and his friend Donald Klopfer purchased the Modern Library from Liveright in 1925, the two created Random House Publishing. Soon, Random House grew into one of the biggest publishers in the industry. In 1933 Horace Liveright died, and Boni & Liveright was absorbed into W. W. Norton. The old Boni & Liveright building, on the corner of Sixth Avenue and West 48th Street, was knocked down in 1930 to make way for Rockefeller Center. Next door to it was another publisher from the era, Simon & Schuster, which remains today in the same location.

Passwords, Scotch, and the Dog under the Table: Dorothy and the Speaks

Dorothy Parker may have lunched at the Algonquin Hotel, but her nightlife was at the speakeasy. She whiled away many a Jazz Age night at the drinking holes of Manhattan.

During the 1920s, at gin joints such as Jack and Charlie's and Tony Soma's, Dorothy lived the high life as one of the era's leading personalities. Carousing into the morning hours with her husband Eddie, Robert Benchley, Scott and Zelda Fitzgerald, or one of her boyfriends, she would bring her dog and set him under her chair; if he stirred, she'd slip him half a sleeping pill. Even while sipping drinks and exchanging banter, Dorothy was always observing, noting each detail and imprinting the bits of dialogue that gave her work such life and power.

Jack and Charlie's, 42 West 49th Street [7], was run by two cousins, Jack Kriendler and Charlie Berns. They got their start with their West Village speakeasy, the Red Head, in 1922. Their illegal club inside a tea room was an immediate hit. In 1925, at the height of the bootlegging era, they moved the speakeasy to a basement at 88 Washington Place.[5] Called the Fronton, it had a small bar, live jazz, and a kitchen. Among the regulars was the poet Edna St. Vincent Millay, whom Dorothy acknowledged as an influence on her own work. The cousins' wild success forced them to relocate to 42 West 49th Street, where a row of nondescript brownstones hid speakeasies, brothels, and gambling dens.

The business moved uptown in 1927, and the Algonquin crowd became Jack and Charlie's regulars. The speakeasy had a big iron gate, a peephole, and the best booze available on the black market. The cousins served liquor that came from rumrunners avoiding the Coast Guard blockade, never the home-brewed stuff available in less-refined saloons. Nicknamed the Puncheon, it became one of the most popular speaks in town, but only those known to the house or personally introduced by a Jack and Charlie's regular customer were allowed in. Regulars were apt to bump into Parker, Robert Benchley, Alexander Woollcott, Heywood Broun, Franklin P. Adams, Edna Ferber, H. L. Mencken, Will Rogers, F. Scott Fitzgerald, John O'Hara, Ernest Hemingway, and any number of actors, ballplayers, and Yale men. It was at Jack and Charlie's that Parker spent the evening in 1928 after her divorce from Eddie was finalized: Dorothy was drinking with her current boyfriend, John Garrett II, and crying her eyes out.

The club was hardly affected by the stock market crash of October 1929, even though its patrons lost millions. The bar owners extended credit to their hard-up clients and issued scrip to use on the premises. On December 31, 1929, a raucous New Year's Eve party literally tore the place up, and with good reason: Rockefeller Center was going to be built on the spot that Jack and Charlie's occupied. Regulars, including Benchley, wielded pickaxes and hammers on the place and began the destruction. Then the crowd, some lugging pieces of the old place, marched uptown three blocks to where the cousins would reopen as "21," at 21 West 52nd Street. The address of Jack and Charlie's was wiped out by Rockefeller Center, but its general vicinity is now occupied by Christie's auction house.

Dorothy also spent a lot of time imbibing at **Tony Soma's**, across the street from Jack and Charlie's, at **[8] 45 West 49th Street**. At Tony's, Mrs. Parker and Mr. Benchley were able to engage in the type of hijinks they were so famous for. For example, amused by a patron showing off his new "indestructible" watch, the pair took delight in pounding the hell out of it, stomping on it, and handing it back to the owner. "It's stopped," he said. They answered together, "Maybe you wound it too tight!"

Gordon Kahn and Al Hirschfeld's *The Speakeasies of 1932* depicts Tony's as both devilish and delightful:

> With few exceptions the women who frequent the place are sloppy drinkers. You can tell the hardier female guzzlers because they sit at the bar. . . . Usually a representation of ladies on the loose at tea time, and flirtations with them aren't difficult. . . . Carlos is the bartender. A dull-witted Basque, he is slow on the uptake, uninspired in his work with the shaker and bottle. . . . Straight, hard liquor and cocktails are a dollar. . . . The bar is small, but complete. The brandy, fair. The Bacardis, good.[6]

Tony's suffered the same fate as Jack and Charlie's: Rockefeller Center's wrecking ball. In 1930 it closed and moved to 59 West 52nd Street, on the same block as "21." The seventy-story Radio Corporation of America building, completed in May 1933, sits on the spot where the original Tony's was located. This is now the headquarters of NBC, where *Saturday Night Live* and *The Today Show* are produced. Seventy stories above Tony's old spot is the building's observation deck. This is a fantastic place to get a 360-degree view of the city, including Central Park.

The Ultimate Social Scene

One of the most famous restaurants in the United States was also one of the most popular watering holes for Dorothy Parker and her crowd during the thirties. **[9] "21," 21 West 52nd Street**, was a step back to a time when bartenders wore white coats and the mixing of a cocktail was handled like a religious ceremony. For nearly a century, books, plays, and movies have been produced about "21." Bar patrons reveled in its time machine aura: collectibles, model airplanes, toy trucks, baseball mitts, football helmets, *New Yorker* cartoons, antique bar signs, a ship's bell, and more. Its exterior was lined with statuettes of colorful jockeys, representing the stables of "21" regulars.

One day in the 1930s, after the Round Table had disbanded and Dorothy was married to Alan Campbell, she and Benchley found themselves at "21" discussing their own relationship. According to one account, she asked her best friend, "Why don't we get married right now?" "What would we do with Alan?" Benchley asked. "Send him to military school," she replied.

In November 1945, Benchley died at age fifty-six from a cerebral hemorrhage, and the club, which had been one of his favorites, hosted an informal wake. Marc Connelly and a group of Benchley's friends gathered at "21" and fortified themselves with scotch in a private room upstairs. At 6 p.m. Connelly put in a call to Dorothy, living in Los Angeles, who was organizing the simultaneous West Coast tribute dinner at the movie star haven Chasen's, on the corner of Beverly Boulevard and Doheny Drive.

"We're here," Connelly told Dorothy. "Now, Dorothy, if you all will raise your glasses . . ."

Dorothy cut him off. "Raise our glasses?" she said. "Why, Marc, you stupid bastard, it's only three o'clock here, and we're all at work. I meant West Coast time, you silly son of a bitch."

A plaque in the bar, to Benchley's memory, simply says, "Robert Benchley—His Corner." Sadly, "21" was closed by new owners LVMH in 2020.

Bathtub Gin Party Place

When Dorothy and her pals were tossed out of a speakeasy at closing time, they would head to [10] the **Knickerbocker Hotel, 1466 Broadway**. Dorothy brought Charlie MacArthur, her boyfriend at the time, to a Broadway cocktail party here in the winter of 1923. He had a wife somewhere else, but Dorothy didn't care. He also got her pregnant; after her abortion she quipped, "That's what you get for putting all your eggs in one bastard."

At a Knickerbocker party, Neysa McMein met Jack Baragwanath, a divorced mining engineer. Neysa played the piano while the rest of the crowd sang along. Not long after the party, Neysa and Jack secretly married. Before Dorothy and Charlie split, they suffered the indignity of being caught together by federal agents in a speakeasy raid.

The fifteen-story Knickerbocker was opened in October 1906 by John Jacob Astor IV, who also built the St. Regis and the original Waldorf-Astoria on 34th Street. It was one of the finest offerings from the era of lavish dining, with large hotel orchestras and ballroom dancing. When the Knickerbocker opened, New York's theater district had recently moved to Longacre Square, renamed Times Square when the newspaper moved to 42nd Street in 1904. The hotel was favored by Broadway stars such as George M. Cohan, and Enrico Caruso was a frequent guest. When the Armistice was declared on November 11, 1918, the Italian tenor sang to a crowd gathered underneath his window.

60 | Dorothy Parker's New York

The Knickerbocker, with its beaux arts, red brick, terracotta caravansary details and eye-catching copper mansard roof, looks much as it did a century ago. The hotel's glory ended in the 1920s, however, when it was closed and converted to offices. The ground floor, where the palatial lobby once was located, has been given over completely to retail shops. In 2015, the hotel reopened as a luxury destination with a roof terrace bar and restaurant, St. Cloud, that has sweeping views of Times Square. The hotel lays claim to inventing the martini, an urban legend.

Hell's Kitchen Parties

Jane Grant and Harold Ross bought **[11] 412 West 47th Street** in September 1923. The duplex was too large for the couple, so they sought friends to move into the building with them and share costs. Among the communal residents was the iconoclastic drama

Figure 23. This Hell's Kitchen location is where *The New Yorker* was created. The parties here attracted celebrities from across New York. *Source:* Photo by the author.

critic Aleck Woollcott. He and Ross had met in Paris during the war and worked on an army newspaper together. Through the following years, they remained close friends and fellow Round Tablers.

When Grant and Ross moved into the house, Parker, Charlie MacArthur (who would go on to write the hit play *The Front Page*), and Harpo Marx hired a street carousel to entertain the neighborhood kids. Charlie stood outside the house, passing out handbills inviting passersby inside for a party. At the star-studded housewarming party, Robert Benchley was talked into performing his hit monologue "The Treasurer's Report" for the crowd.

The Ross-Grant-Woollcott house was the scene of scores of legendary parties and after-theater gatherings. Parker was a frequent visitor and so were the other Vicious Circle members, as well as Ethel Barrymore, Scott and Zelda Fitzgerald, and George Gershwin, who performed "Rhapsody in Blue" on their piano. So much booze was brought into the house by bootleggers that the neighbors thought there was a speakeasy in the building. Grant made her own bathtub gin. The home was the spot of marathon poker parties. In 1924 the house was given over to launching *The New Yorker*.

The home was converted to individual apartments decades ago. A perennial "for rent" sign hangs on the sad exterior of this literary landmark.

Not Much Fun

Dorothy was often the life of the party, even when her own life was no bowl of maraschino cherries. When the bartender at Tony Soma's greeted her arrival in the bar with "What are you having?" she replied without missing a beat, "Not much fun." This classic Parker rejoinder provokes rueful laughter while laying bare the truth of her personal life: While she had some wild nights on the town and glamorous boyfriends in the twenties, these years were also a shallow and often difficult time. She bounced from apartment to apartment throughout the decade, just as she bounced from lover to lover. The trail of residences begins on the Upper West Side, where Dorothy became Mrs. Parker.

The Honeymoon Is Over

In 1918, when Dorothy was twenty-four and on the staff of *Vanity Fair*, she took a furnished apartment on **[12] West 71st Street**, just one street away from the house she

62 | Dorothy Parker's New York

lived in as a child, at 214 West 72nd Street. Maybe she wanted the security of living in the old neighborhood because she would be living here alone while her husband, Eddie, was in the army.

This is the kind of apartment that a solitary woman, whose husband is away in the army, occupies in stories such as "The Lovely Leave" (1943) and the poem "The Small Hours" (1926):

No more my little song comes back;
 And now of nights I lay
My head on down, to watch the black
 And wait the unfailing gray.

Oh, sad are winter nights, and slow;
 And sad's a song that's dumb;
And sad it is to lie and know
 Another dawn will come.[7]

After Eddie returned from the war, the couple lived here together until 1920. This apartment proved too glum for them, though, so the couple eventually moved—not too far, however.

Dorothy and Eddie on the Skids

The postwar Parkers didn't get along for a variety of reasons. Whereas Dorothy was a discerning drama critic with impossibly high standards, her husband preferred the "leg and fanny shows" that were popular at the time. No match for the wits at the Round Table, he became the butt of many of Dorothy's jokes. Eddie returned to his job in finance. Meanwhile, his wife was becoming a national celebrity.

In February 1920, just a few weeks after Dorothy was dropped by *Vanity Fair*, a national census taker found the couple living at **[13] 252 West 76th Street**, a few doors west of Broadway. They were in one of the many upscale apartments on the Upper West Side. Both were listed as "boarders" in the building—Dorothy in room 834 and Eddie in room 704. Her occupation was listed as "Writer, magazines," and his was "Broker." The couple moved to West 57th Street not long after this, but a change of apartments could not help this marriage.

Drink and Dance and Laugh and Lie | 63

Bad Marriage, Bad Apartment

Dorothy and Eddie Parker spent their unhappiest times at **[14] 57 West 57th Street**. The building is on the corner of one of the busiest streets in Midtown.

Their love for each other fading, the couple resided here briefly in the early 1920s while they struggled to stay together. Dorothy used her time here to mine for future stories and verse.

In those days, the Sixth Avenue subway was elevated, not underground like it is today. This was a noisy, sooty street, and the Parkers would have had to shout to be heard at times—and shout they did. They had a rented flat on the top floor of the shabby three-story, red-brick building. The building was really a commercial property for artists

Figure 24. This is Park Row, also nicknamed Newspaper Row, around 1905. From left to right are City Hall, the *New York World* (Pulitzer Building), *New York Sun*, the *New York Tribune* (with tower), the *New York Times*, and the American Tract Society Building. Dorothy Parker's writing was printed in the *World*, the *Tribune*, and the *Times*. *Source:* Detroit Publishing Company, Library of Congress, Prints and Photographs Division.

who needed studio space but lived elsewhere. It must have been dreary with the train running practically on top of it—certainly no place for a writer. Yet, Dorothy managed to write pieces there for *Life*, the *Saturday Evening Post*, and *Ladies' Home Journal*.

Another resident of the building was Neysa McMein, who became a friend of Parker and painted her portrait in 1922. The Round Tablers often came to McMein's studio for drinks while she painted. Notable sculptor Sally James Farnham also had a studio here. Downstairs was the Swiss Alps, a restaurant that sent dinners up to Dorothy, who couldn't even boil an egg.

The Parkers separated in 1922 and took another six years to finalize their divorce. They were probably among the last tenants of the building on West 57th, which was knocked down in the late twenties for the bedazzled office building that still stands there.

Dorothy in Distress

One of Parker's love affairs in the mid-1920s was with Seward "Sewie" Collins, a friend of Edmund Wilson's from Princeton. Collins had a brief magazine career until he bought a small literary publication, *The Bookman*. He used his position as publisher to woo Dorothy, who become enamored with him, to the point of giving him first crack at two of her most famous stories: "A Telephone Call" (January 1928) and "Big Blonde" (February 1929). After carrying on a rocky and turbulent relationship with Collins for months, by early 1927 Dorothy was exhausted. On March 25, her sister Helen sent a one-sentence telegram to Collins, which was delivered to him at the Breakers in Palm Beach: "*Dorothy very ill heart and nerve prostration due to your telegram please send her nice message.*"[8] Over the course of that winter, Collins had gone from Paris to Palm Beach and on to Pasadena, California, to get away from the fragile writer. Dorothy, unable to recover from yet another failed romance, checked into **[15] Presbyterian Hospital**, at **41 East 70th Street**, between Park and Madison avenues. Four days later, Collins was handed another telegram, this one from Dorothy, as he lounged at the luxury hotel:

> *Seems heart has sprung leak own volition. Would have several little Dutch boys hold their thumbs there. But they say must be long rest here and then can only be half person never one of boys again. Guess that was not so important was it. . . . Doctor working with me mentally and don't mean Christian Science or analysis. Trying to get me out of sense of shame that blocks work like stone wall. Maybe someday can be useful and even self-respecting person. Promise never send you blue word again. But now seems long road ahead. Your friendship loveliest thing. Please let me be confident of it.*[9]

Presbyterian Hospital was founded in 1868 by James Lenox, a prominent New Yorker who also helped establish the New York Public Library with John Jacob Astor. In 1997 the hospital merged with New York Hospital, the second-oldest hospital in the country, which had opened in 1771 under an English royal charter granted by King George III. Today, the site of the former Presbyterian Hospital is a luxury residence.

Working through Writer's Block

While living at the Algonquin Hotel in February 1932, Parker attempted suicide by swallowing barbiturates. She was distraught over her most recent breakup with her young playboy companion John McClain. Though she had recently published a third collection of verse, *Death and Taxes*, which was selling well, privately she referred to the preceding twelve months as "this year of hell."

In an attempt to turn her life around, Dorothy left the Algonquin suite and took a furnished apartment at **[16]** the **Lowell**, at **28 East 63rd Street**. This was yet another residential hotel apartment; she favored this sort of apartment because she had few (if any) domestic skills, possessed no furniture, and traveled frequently. The seventeen-story building came with maid service, a fully equipped kitchen—which Dorothy ignored—a working wood-burning fireplace, and a terrace.

After moving into the Lowell, Dorothy produced some of the best short stories of her career. She would ask friends to come over and sit with her for three or four hours and force her to stay focused and keep writing. While the friends occupied themselves, Dorothy sat and labored over her desk, writing in longhand. Among the classics from this period are "Lady with a Lamp," "Dusk before Fireworks," "Horsie," and "The Waltz," all of which were published between 1932 and 1933 in *Harper's Bazaar* or *The New Yorker*. Dorothy was forced to keep writing because she was broke. The Lowell, a fairly new art deco building, was quite beyond her means, but the managers let her stay because they liked the publicity that came with having a famous writer in residence.

Today the Lowell is a luxury boutique hotel, catering to those who enjoy an exclusive setting that will costs thousands of dollars for one's head to hit the pillow. When Madonna lived there for nine months, she asked the management to convert part of her suite into a private gym. They complied.

New Leaf, New Life, and Good-Bye, NYC

The year 1933 was a turning point in Dorothy Parker's life. With the nation deep in the Depression, the Algonquin Round Table long gone, and her close friends scattered to the winds, Dorothy was about to abandon her familiar lifestyle.

That year, at age forty-one, Dorothy was introduced to Alan Campbell, a thirty-year-old bit-part actor and writer from Virginia. At the time, she had all but ceased writing verse, completing only two or three pieces a year. She'd spent two years living in Switzerland with Gerald and Sara Murphy and was floating through New York parties and social events. When Alan got a part in a play, she left the Lowell and rented an apartment at **[17] 444 East 52nd Street** with him.

The red-brick apartment, built in 1929, is between Sutton Place and Beekman Place—one of the poshest spots in the city. Parker complained that it was "far enough east to plant tea," but across the street was Aleck Woollcott's apartment (which she had dubbed Wit's End), so she was close to at least one former member of the Round Table. When she and Alan moved in together, they adopted two dogs, Bedlington terriers named Wolf and Cora, neither of which they bothered to train.

While living here, Dorothy and Alan socialized with John O'Hara, Adele and Robert A. Lovett, and Sara and Gerald Murphy. Ernest Hemingway was in their circle when he was in the city. Dorothy also spent time with Scott Fitzgerald while he was getting ready to publish his masterpiece *Tender Is the Night*, which featured characters based on the Murphys. At the time, Zelda was at a treatment facility on the Hudson, and Scott and Dorothy painted the town in her absence.

In early 1934 Dorothy made appearances on Woollcott's CBS radio show *The Town Crier* while deciding what to do next. When Alan joined a summer stock theater company in Denver, they packed up the dogs and went West. After being hounded by reporters about their relationship, the couple tied the knot in a civil ceremony in Raton, New Mexico. Once the season ended at the Elitch Gardens in Denver, they bought a Ford flivver and kept on going West to Hollywood to begin a screenwriting career.

Today, the magnificent art deco gem where they ended their New York chapter appears not to have aged. It is ten stories tall and capped with three stone thunderbirds, quoins, and fine decorative details. This quiet street is a dead end, overlooking the edge of the island, FDR Drive, and the East River, and it looks much the same as when Parker and Fitzgerald tumbled out of a taxicab there in the 1930s.

Drink and Dance and Laugh and Lie | 67

4

The Aisle Seat

Dorothy Parker as Theater Critic

Some of the most colorful chapters in Dorothy Parker's life were written during her tenure as a drama critic, first at *Vanity Fair*, where she made her reputation as the only female theater critic on Broadway, and later at *Ainslee's* and *The New Yorker*. She was certainly not the fairest or most kindhearted reviewer, but few critics have surpassed her wit in the years since she first took up the aisle seat.

When *Vanity Fair* drama critic P. G. "Plum" Wodehouse told Frank Crowninshield that he was taking a leave of absence, the editor did not cast a wide net for a replacement. He had known Dorothy since 1914. She had come to his staff after more than two years at *Vogue*, working her way up to more important writing and editing chores. Some touch of editorial genius prompted Crownie to give his office wisecracker the job as drama critic. So what if all she knew about live theater was what she had observed as a paying customer? For him to put all his faith and trust in her was a big step considering that at the time *Vanity Fair* was a publishing sensation. She took on the role in Spring 1918 and lasted until early 1920.

After leaving the employ of *Vanity Fair*, Parker was snapped up by the editors at *Ainslee's*, who promptly installed her as drama critic. The next move brought Mrs. Parker to a much wider national audience. At *Vanity Fair*, the average monthly circulation in 1919 was approximately 68,000. Beginning in May 1920, Dorothy Parker readers could find her theater reviews *Ainslee's*. Its average circulation at the time was about 773,000.

Figure 25. Seeing double: Dorothy Parker enjoying tea with advice columnist and "sob sister" Dorothy Dix (real name Elizabeth Meriwether Gilmer). Dix was both the highest-paid and most widely read female newspaper writer of the Jazz Age, with an audience of more than sixty million readers. *Source:* Dorothy Parker Society Archives.

Ainslee's at one time was one of the biggest publishers of fiction in America, rivaled only by *Harper's*. *Ainslee's* essentially invented the monthly short story magazine format.

This monthly magazine, which began in the 1890s, published fiction by some of the greats of the early twentieth century: Stephen Crane, Theodore Dreiser, Bret Harte, O. Henry, and Jack London. Her column "In Broadway Playhouses" first appeared in May 1920, and she reviewed shows monthly through the middle of 1923, when the magazine started to run out of steam shortly before it folded.

Parker took a break from dramatic criticism for eight years; it took her dear friend Robert Benchley to lure her back. From February to April 1931 she substituted for him while he worked on motion picture shorts, writing a weekly column for *The New Yorker*.

Parker produced a monthly column for five years, from 1918 to 1923, attending as many as six shows a week. She witnessed the opening nights of classics by Eugene O'Neill, reviewed Al Jolson in blackface, and saw Will Rogers and W. C. Fields become stars. She used her powers of observation to isolate the small but telling details of a performance, from the make of a dress to the speed of a speech. However, even at her dismissive best (as in her demolition of the play *The House Beautiful* at the Apollo Theater), Dorothy's love and understanding of the theater was clear—it was just that her standards were so high. For example, in her January 1919 review of *Tiger! Tiger!* at the Belasco, Dorothy waxed nostalgic for an earlier time (which, for her, meant primarily the days of Maude Adams as Peter Pan) and declared the current state of the theater to be in crisis:

> Often, in those long quiet hours when I am caught in a subway block, or sitting in the dentist's antechamber, or waiting for a Broadway car, I ponder sadly on the good old times that have passed beyond recall. Those were the happy days—the days when people rushed gladly to the theater, enjoyed every minute of it, applauded enthusiastically, wished there were more, and came out wreathed in smiles to spread abroad the glad tidings that "The show was great!" Why, some of them even, of their own free will, went back to see the same play over and over again. Yes, those were undoubtedly the days. Think how hideously different things are now. We go heroically to the theater, hoping always, with piteous faith, that maybe it won't be so bad after all—yet ever dreading, with the bitter fear born of cruel experience, that probably it will be worse.[1]

This was a bold statement for a twenty-five-year-old rookie in her second year as New York's only female theater critic, but this was the way Dorothy did everything: without pulling any punches. It is part of why she held such an important position in the energetic and exciting world of New York theater.

Broadway during the 1910s and 1920s was quite different from what it is today. Close to eighty theaters were in operation, with as many as seven shows debuting on the same night. Without competition from talking pictures or television, live theater was the most popular form of public entertainment available.

When Dorothy began her career as a critic, it was a heady time on Broadway. Ethel Barrymore was onstage; the first Pulitzer Prize for drama was awarded to Jesse Lynch Williams for the comedy *Why Marry?* Over at the musical theaters, audiences could see twenty-six-year-old Brooklyn native Mae West at the Shubert; Al Jolson, Marilyn Miller, and Fred and Adele Astaire at the Winter Garden; and Will Rogers and W. C. Fields at the New Amsterdam in the Ziegfeld *Follies*.

After World War II many of the old Broadway theaters were razed to make way for new development. During the "Broadway Massacre" in 1982, five old theaters were knocked down together in order to build the Marriott Marquis hotel. Today, however,

The Aisle Seat | 71

Figure 26. Times Square in 1928, when there were blockbuster shows every night. The Marx Brothers were in *Animal Crackers*, and audiences could see Eddie Cantor, W. C. Fields, Al Jolson, Marilyn Miller, and Mae West. *Source:* Public Domain.

the business of Broadway is robust again. In the 1983 to 1984 season, 8.7 million tickets were sold, for a box office revenue of $230 million, according to the League of American Theatres and Producers. Forty years later, the 2023 season saw 12,283,399 tickets sold, earning $1.6 billion.

Since Dorothy's Broadway days, though, the number of productions has dropped dramatically; in the early twenties there were seventy-seven theaters in operation; today there are about forty. The 1929 to 1930 season had 233 productions; by the next season, due to Hollywood's siren call and the Great Depression, that number sank to 187 productions; in 1939 there were 98. The 2023 season saw only 23 new Broadway shows.

Figure 27. Map of the Theater District showing old Broadway theaters. *Source:* Collection of the author.

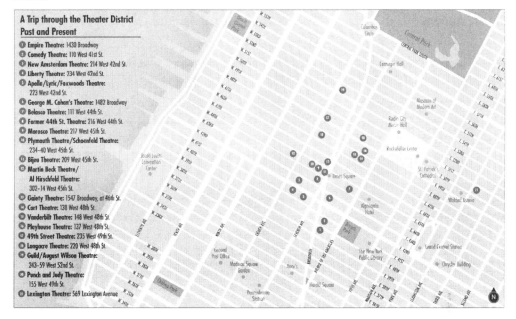

[1] Empire Theatre

1430 Broadway. Opened 1893; demolished 1953.

The Empire played a central role in Dorothy's development as a theater critic. She had watched *Peter Pan* here in 1906 as an enthralled twelve-year-old. In December 1918 she returned to review another James M. Barrie play, *Dear Brutus*. It lasted 184 performances—only a modest success—but Dorothy, writing for *Vanity Fair*, had high praise for the leading lady: "The ladies' cup goes to Helen Hayes, who does an exquisite bit of acting . . . she never once skips over to the kittenish, never once grows too exuberantly sweet. . . . I could sit down right now and fill reams of paper with a single-spaced list of the names of actresses who could have completely spoiled the part." In a twist, Parker's erstwhile boyfriend, Charlie MacArthur, left his wife and married an actress he had met at Neysa McMein's studio: Hayes.

Parker returned to the Empire Theatre again and again. Reviewing in Benchley's stead, she caught *The Barretts of Wimpole Street* in February 1931 then announced in the pages of *The New Yorker*, "If you want to, you can pick me out of any crowd, these days. I am the little one in the corner who did not think that *The Barretts of Wimpole Street* was a great play, nor even a good play. It is true that I paid it the tribute of tears, but that says nothing, for I am one who weeps at Victorian costumes."

[2] Comedy Theatre

110 West 41st Street. Opened 1909; demolished 1942.

Parker visited the Comedy in September 1918 for a production of Oscar Wilde's *An Ideal Husband*. Writing for *Vanity Fair*, Dorothy quickly pinpointed the flaws in one actor's performance: "Norman Trevor, as Sir Robert Chiltern, seems to have adopted a new technique; the idea is to see how quickly he can get through his speeches. He broke all previously existing world's records in the second-act tirade about women's love."

Because it had only 623 seats, the Comedy was considered too small for musicals or major productions, but among its famous tenants were Orson Welles and John Houseman's Mercury Players in the late 1930s. The Comedy fell victim to World War II–era expansion in the Times Square area, and now business offices stand in the space.

Figure 28. The New Amsterdam Theatre is the longtime home of Disney musicals. It is said to be haunted by the ghost of Olive Thomas, a *Follies* star who died tragically at age twenty-five. *Source:* Library of Congress, Prints and Photographs Division.

[3] New Amsterdam Theatre

214 West 42nd Street. Opened 1903.

The New Amsterdam is one of the oldest theaters still in use today. In 1913, Flo Ziegfeld moved his *Follies* to the theater. The chorus girls were a smash hit, and the annual revue was a sensation. In 1924 humorist Will Rogers was in the cast when he wrote an article for the *Times* about the *Follies*. "Was with Flo Ziegfeld this morning," Rogers wrote. "The present show in our old *Follies* theatre, the New Amsterdam, was raided by the police yesterday. He says show business is getting pretty tough when you have to guarantee a raid with each ticket."

While writing for *The New Yorker* in March 1931, Dorothy walked over to 42nd Street to review *The Admirable Crichton* by James M. Barrie, which lasted fewer than sixty performances. She wrote, "I have, happily for me, never before seen upon one stage so many discourteous, patronizing, and exaggerated performances . . . all my envy goes out to Mr. Walter Winchell, who walked wanly out into the foyer after the third act . . . and summed up the whole thing in the phrase, 'Well, for Crichton out loud!'"

The New Amsterdam, which celebrated its centennial in 2003, has a narrow, beaux arts–inspired facade and a vertical sign that went up in 1937 when it was used as a movie house. The theater closed in 1985 and was reopened by the Walt Disney Company in 1997. The interior has amazing art nouveau decor, and the lobby, stairwells, and auditorium feature ornate terracotta panels.

[4] Liberty Theatre

234 West 42nd Street. Opened 1904; closed 1933.

The Liberty Theatre and *Caesar's Wife*, produced by Florenz Ziegfeld Jr., proved to be Dorothy's undoing at *Vanity Fair*. The star was Billie Burke, Ziegfeld's second wife. The play, written by Somerset Maugham, lasted less than three months, thanks in part to Dorothy's review of a November 1919 performance: "Miss Burke is at her best in her more serious moments; in her desire to convey the girlishness of her character, she plays her lighter scenes rather as if she were giving an impersonation of Eva Tanguay." It was this comparison to a bawdy vaudeville star of the time (or perhaps, as some claimed, the description of Burke's ankles as thick) that provoked Ziegfeld to complain to Condé Nast. The result: Parker was soon dismissed from the magazine.

Dorothy gave Flo a poke in the ribs in 1922 in a series called "Life's Valentines" for *Life*:

The Aisle Seat | 75

Still we're groggy from the blow
Dealt us—by the famous Flo;
After 1924,
He announces, nevermore
Will his shows our senses greet—
At a cost of five per seat.
Hasten, Time, your onward drive—
Welcome, 1925![2]

The Liberty Theatre, was open from 1904 to 1933 and then converted to a movie theater. In 2000 the building was gutted to house Madame Tussauds Wax Museum. Inside are wax figures of Dorothy Parker and F. Scott Fitzgerald.

Figure 29. Billie Burke had a four-decade acting career and only outlived Dorothy Parker by three years. *Source:* Bain News Service, Library of Congress, Prints and Photographs Division.

[5] Apollo/Lyric Theatre

223 West 42nd Street. Opened 1910 and 1903; renovated 1996.

Parker wrote her most succinctly devastating review after seeing a new play written by Channing Pollock, *The House Beautiful*, at the Apollo in March 1931. Her seven-word *chiasmus* stands as one of her most-quoted reviews: "*The House Beautiful* is the play lousy." The Apollo, built in 1910, and the Lyric Theatre, built in 1903, stood side by side on 42nd Street. For decades both were classic old-time Broadway houses, only to later suffer the indignity of life as X-rated theaters. In 1996 the Apollo and Lyric were gutted and combined into one large theater. Significant architectural elements and the facade were retained and restored. The new Lyric seats 1,622.

The old Lyric Theatre entrance at 214 West 43rd Street has three busts above the doorway, a link to the theater's origins in musicals. The sculptures are of the light opera composer Reginald De Koven, for whom the theater was built, and Victorian-era composers W. S. Gilbert and Arthur Sullivan.

[6] George M. Cohan's Theatre

1482 Broadway. Opened 1911; demolished 1938.

Heywood Broun was one of Parker's all-time favorite people. A popular columnist at the *New York World*, in 1931 he produced an ill-fated musical called *Shoot the Works* at George M. Cohan's Theatre. His grand idea was to give work to struggling performers as the Depression set in. It opened on July 21, 1931, and ran for eighty-seven performances. The revue tapped the talents of many, including Peter Arno, Irving Berlin, Dorothy Fields, Ira Gershwin, and Parker herself: a skit from Dorothy's short story "You Were Perfectly Fine" was included. The show had created so much buzz it attracted Al Hirschfeld to draw it for the *Herald-Tribune*.

Alexander Woollcott didn't want to review a show with his friends in it; however, he did want a part in it, although he didn't get one. Dorothy's participation was a summertime diversion, but Broun cast the chorus girls himself (later he married one, Connie Madison). Broun sang, danced, and acted in the show.

The theater opened in 1911, boasting more than a thousand seats. Artwork in the lobby celebrated the vaudeville history of Cohan's theater-loving family. In 1932 it was converted to a movie house, but it struggled because of its close proximity to the Roxy, Rialto, Paramount, State, Rivoli, Strand, and others. In 1938 it was demolished to make way for retail stores.

Figure 30. The Belasco Theatre was known for realism in productions. David Belasco once told his carpenters to rent a room at a brothel, then actually dismantle the room, carry it out of the building, and put it onto the stage. *Source:* Photo by the author.

[7] Belasco Theatre

111 West 44th Street. Opened 1907.

Dorothy had her knitting needles out when she walked into the Belasco Theatre to see *Tiger! Tiger!* in November 1918. This stinker, produced by David Belasco and written by Edward Knoblauch, lasted for more than 180 performances—much to Parker's chagrin. In her review for *Vanity Fair*, she roasted the drama: "There is *Tiger! Tiger!* Edward Knoblauch's drama at the Belasco, for instance. Somehow, I cannot feel that the dizzy whirl of modern life had anything to do with my intense suffering during the performance—I hold the play directly responsible."

The Belasco opened in 1907 as the Stuyvesant, but in 1910 playwright, manager, actor, and director David Belasco bought it and renamed it. He spared no expense, and it was a marvel of modern stagecraft when it opened as the Belasco, with innovations in lighting and an elevator stage. Belasco, who dressed in the black garb of a priest, was hardly saintly. For his leading ladies, Belasco installed a private backstage elevator that ascended to his luxury apartment above the theater. One of the oldest theaters still in use on Broadway, it has landmark status and offers tours of its inner workings.

Dorothy wrote a "valentine" to Belasco, printed in *Life* in February 1922:

Often in the local press
On your kindness you lay stress.
Love's the basis of your art,
So you say—that is, in part.
Frequently you tell us of
How devotedly you love
Actors, public, critics, too . . .
Echo answers, "Yes, you do."

[8] 44th Street Theatre

216 West 44th Street. Opened 1912; demolished 1945.

The date: New Year's Eve, 1928. The place: the 44th Street Theatre. The occasion: the hit show *Animal Crackers*, starring the Marx Brothers. Nearly every Algonquin Round Table member attended the performance and then went out to ring in 1929 together. The show was written by George S. Kaufman and Morrie Ryskind. It starred Groucho (Captain Spalding), Chico (Emanuel Ravelli), Harpo (the Professor), and Zeppo (Jamison). Harpo was close to Alexander Woollcott, who brought the brothers to the attention of his friends.

The theater, built in 1912, had its last show in 1945: *On the Town*, with music by Leonard Bernstein. This is also where the Stage Door Canteen was located during World War II—a restaurant and bar for servicemen, where celebrities would drop in and entertain the boys. It was demolished soon after, when the *New York Times* extended its building from 43rd Street.

[9] Morosco Theatre

217 West 45th Street. Opened 1917; demolished 1982.

The Morosco Theatre, with more than 900 seats, was named for impresario Oliver Morosco. When Parker went to the Morosco in September 1919 to write for *Ainslee's*, she witnessed a popular trend of the season, the Great War comedy:

Civilian Clothes, written by Thompson Buchanan and presented at the Morosco, with Olive Tell and Thurston Hall in the leading rôles, is a welcome idea in comedies. The heroine, carried away by the glorious olive drab, marries an officer at the front; the blow falls when, back in America, he appears in his Sears Roebucks. Worse, he becomes a butler in her father's house. Of course, you guess all the time that he really doesn't have to be a butler—they never do—that he's just doing it for some obscure reason dealing with showing everyone how wrong they are and how noble he is, but anyway, it all ends beautifully. Unfortunately, the ending naturally came at 10:45, so Mr. Morosco whiled away the remaining fifteen minutes by adding a totally unnecessary bedroom scene, which does all it can to spoil the evening. If he can't consciously feel that the audience should leave before eleven, Mr. Morosco might far better fill in the time by showing lantern slides of Our Giant California Redwoods, or by employing Nate Leipsic to do coin tricks.

Figure 31. Both the facade and the auditorium interior of the Gerald Schoenfeld Theatre are designated New York City landmarks. *Source:* Photo by the author.

The Morosco, known for drama and comedies, met the wrecking ball with the Bijou and other nearby theaters in 1982 to enable construction of the Marriott Marquis Hotel.

[10] Plymouth/Schoenfeld Theatre

234–40 West 45th Street. Opened 1917.

Parker saw many shows at the Plymouth, among them Ibsen's *Hedda Gabler* in April 1918, not long after it opened. In *Vanity Fair* Dorothy proclaimed the play's importance: "After *Hedda Gabler*, the season was over for me. There just wasn't one other thing that I could get all heated up about. My life was a long succession of thin evenings." She also was in the audience for Leo Tolstoy's *Redemption* in October 1918. As she wrote in *Vanity Fair*, this play, too, had a dramatic effect on her: "I went into the Plymouth Theatre a comparatively young woman, and I staggered out of it, three hours later, twenty years older, haggard and broken with suffering."

Designed and built by architect Herbert J. Krapp, the Plymouth opened in 1918. The theater's patterned brickwork and its interior, based on the neoclassical designs of Robert Adams, make it a city landmark. In May 2005 it was renamed for Shubert Organization chairman Gerald Schoenfeld.

[11] Bijou Theatre

209 West 45th Street. Opened 1917; demolished 1982.

The long-gone Bijou Theatre has dual ties to Dorothy Parker, as both a critic and a creator. Parker trudged to the Bijou one night in March 1931 to review the play *Lady Beyond the Moon* for *The New Yorker*. She wrote, "It was a dull, silly, dirty play of some sort of house-party on Lake Como." The show lasted barely two weeks.

Three years later she was back to watch an original production of a play based on her material, *After Such Pleasures*. The play, a montage of scenes culled from her short fiction and poetry, was written and directed by Edward F. Gardner and starred Shirley Booth. Although Parker didn't have a hand in the show, she did have a stake in its success and royalties. Unfortunately, it ran for only twenty-three performances after its February 7, 1934, opening.

The Bijou was one of the smaller theaters on Broadway, with only 365 seats. It was designed by Herbert J. Krapp, who also designed the Plymouth and the Broadhurst for the Shuberts. The Bijou opened in 1917 and was a Broadway theater until the 1950s. It changed hands and became CBS Studio 62 in 1951; in 1962 it showed art films as the D. W. Griffith Theatre. It then switched back to being the Bijou Theatre until

Figure 32. The Al Hirschfeld Theatre is named for the most famous Broadway artist. His caricature of himself forms the sign on the marquee. *Source:* Photo by the author.

Godzilla came in 1965, when it became the Toho Cinema, screening Japanese films. It was a movie house until 1982, when, along with the Morosco and three other theaters, it was knocked down.

[17] Martin Beck/Al Hirschfeld Theatre

302–14 West 45th Street. Opened 1924.

Opened in 1924 and named for producer Martin Beck, this is among the most spectacular of Broadway theaters, and its Moorish-Byzantine-inspired interiors and lavish decoration have helped it attain landmark status. Beck, a vaudeville mogul, came up with the concept, which was designed and executed by San Francisco architect G. Albert Lansburgh. The theater features distinctive wrought iron and stained glass. It was renamed after the popular artist Al Hirschfeld in 2003.

It was while exiting through the theater's swinging doors in December 1933 that Parker is reported to have uttered one of her most famous remarks, following Katharine Hepburn's performance as Stella Surrege in an English drawing-room production called *The Lake*: "She ran the gamut of emotions from A to B." When Hepburn passed away in 2003, this quip was mentioned in her *New York Times* obituary.

In the mid-1950s, Lillian Hellman somehow managed to talk Dorothy into providing the lyrics for a musical comedy Hellman was writing, even though Parker was still smarting from the failure of *The Ladies of the Corridor*, a play she had cowritten a few years before. Hellman's project was based on Voltaire's novel *Candide*. Dorothy was asked to write lyrics with Richard Wilbur and John Latouche. The others working on the show were all talented, and it was assumed that this musical would be a big hit. It turned out to be a near miss.

Candide opened on December 1, 1956, at the Martin Beck and ran for 73 performances before the plug was pulled early in 1957. Harold Prince revived it twenty years later, however, and it ran for almost 750 shows; in 1997 it was brought back a third time and ran for another 100. Dorothy knew where to place the blame: "I had only one lyric in it. It didn't work out very well. There were too many geniuses in it, you know."[3]

[13] Gaiety Theatre

1547 Broadway. Opened 1908; closed 1943; demolished 1982.

Like many theater critics, Dorothy Parker thought that if she could review plays, she could write them. In 1924 she teamed up with Elmer Rice, a graduate of New York University Law School who had taken up playwriting instead of law. He had just finished *The Adding Machine* when he agreed to collaborate with Dorothy. Their play, a comedy in three acts about life in dull suburbia and crushed dreams, was initially called *Soft Music* and later renamed *Close Harmony*. It opened at the Gaiety on December 1, 1924, and lasted only twenty-four performances.

The show's lack of success probably ate at Dorothy, but she tried not to show it. After the final afternoon performance, she sent a telegram to Robert Benchley: CLOSE HARMONY DID A COOL NINETY DOLLARS AT THE MATINEE TODAY STOP ASK THE BOYS IN THE BACK ROOM WHAT THEY WILL HAVE. Shrugging off her disappointment, she told her friends, "It was dull. You have my apologies." Her partnership with Rice was more than just artistic; she also slept with him—a performance that came no closer to her standard of perfection. Her review: "the worst f— of my life."

The Gaiety opened in 1908, becoming a silent-movie house in 1926 and then a burlesque theater. It was renamed the Victoria in 1943 and was converted to a movie theater. It became the Embassy Five Theatre in 1978 and was one of five theaters demolished in 1982 to build the Marriott Marquis Hotel.

[14] Cort/James Earl Jones Theatre

138 West 48th Street. Opened 1912.

The Cort, built in 1912 for the producer John Cort, is among the oldest and most beautiful of Broadway theaters. The small, elegant interior is decorated with French neoclassical detail and murals depicting the gardens of Versailles. In December 1919 Dorothy was here for *Vanity Fair* to see John Drinkwater's *Abraham Lincoln*, which had been a big success in London. For this review, Parker showed her rarely seen gentle side:

> The play is so simply written that there is never a suggestion of the theater about it; even such a tried trick as the soft singing of an off-stage army marching off to war somehow loses all theatricalism and becomes grippingly real, so naturally and quietly is it brought in. The management has introduced the same unseen soldiers in another selection, during a scene in Grant's headquarters at Appomattox, and, though it would seem as if, according to the managerial idea, the Union Army was composed of two tenors and a couple of basses, the effect is none the less telling.

Well-known shows presented at the Cort include *The Diary of Anne Frank*, *Sarafina!*, and *The Heiress*. In 2022, following a $47 million expansion-renovation, the theater was renamed by the Shuberts in honor of veteran actor James Earl Jones.

[15] Vanderbilt Theatre

148 West 48th Street. Opened 1918; demolished 1954.

Eugene DeRosa designed the Vanderbilt Theatre, which was known for musicals. In late 1918 Parker paid a visit to review a new play, *The Gentile Wife*, for *Vanity Fair*. The show lasted a month, which was just fine with Dorothy:

From what I could hear of it, I gathered that *The Gentile Wife* is a very interesting play. The actors in Rita Wellman's drama deliver the major part of their speeches with their backs toward the audience, which renders it a bit difficult to gather just what is going on. In fact, I think I should have heard a good deal more of the proceedings if I had left the Vanderbilt Theatre and gone and stood out in the middle of Forty-seventh Street, in which direction they were all facing.

The Vanderbilt opened in March 1918 with the Harry Carroll–Joseph McCarthy musical *Oh Look!* Probably its greatest night was November 2, 1921, when Eugene O'Neill debuted *Anna Christie* on its stage, with Pauline Lord and Frank Shannon in the leads. The 798-seat theater was a popular venue for small plays and musicals until 1939, when it was converted to a radio studio. It reopened briefly in the fifties before being demolished in 1954. In 2008 the Rockefeller Group paid $62 million for the property, at that point a parking garage. A Hampton Inn opened on the spot in 2023 with 1,046 rooms.

[16] Playhouse Theatre

137 West 48th Street. Opened 1911; demolished 1969.

The Phantom Legion, written and produced by Anthony Paul Kelly, opened on December 10, 1919, at the Playhouse. Parker observed in *Vanity Fair*: "Some plays, with an exquisite thoughtfulness, even withdrew, after a brief showing, and resigned their theatres to the incoming entertainments. The outgoing dramas included one curious divertissement called *The Phantom Legion*, which treated of death and the author's astoundingly unattractive conception of an after-life. This play holds the season's record, thus far, with a run of four evening performances and one matinee. By an odd coincidence, it ran just five performances too many."

The Shuberts owned the building from 1944 until it was knocked down in 1969. Today the McGraw-Hill Building stands in its place.

[17] 49th Street Theatre

235 West 49th Street. Opened 1921; demolished 1940.

This theater was the venue for *No Sirree!*—the joint production by the Round Table members. On Sunday, April 30, 1922, "An anonymous entertainment by the Vicious

Circle of the Hotel Algonquin" was put on for one night at the 49th Street Theatre. The entire group—artists, columnists, and critics—wrote and acted in a one-night show for friends. Actors, who had often been the subject of the Round Table's stinging barbs, reviewed the show as guest critics for the major papers.

Dorothy Parker wrote a song called "The Everlastin' Ingénue Blues," which had Helen Hayes and Margalo Gillmore among the chorus. They sang, "We are little flappers, never growing up / And we've all of us been flapping since Belasco was a pup." However, the most popular act of the night was Robert Benchley's "The Treasurer's Report," which prompted Irving Berlin to hire Benchley for his *Music Box Revue*.

While much of the evening's entertainment is lost to history, we do have the text of "The Treasurer's Report," and through it we can catch a glimpse of the tenor of the evening: "I don't think that many members of the Society realize just how big the work is that we are trying to do up there. . . . We feel that, by taking the boy at this age, we can get closer to his real nature—for a boy has a very real nature, you may be sure—and bring him into closer touch not only with the school, the parents, and with each other, but also with the town in which they live, the country to whose flag they pay allegiance, and to the—ah—town in which they live." Benchley's *The Treasurer's Report*, made by Fox-Movietone in 1928, holds the distinction of being the first all-talking movie.

The 49th Street Theatre was built in 1921 for the Shubert Brothers but fell victim to the Depression. It was briefly a movie theater until it was demolished in 1940 to make way for a parking garage. The property was redeveloped; today it is the Pearl Hotel. It opened in October 2010 with ninety-four rooms.

Bonus: Don't miss **St. Malachy Roman Catholic Church** (239 West 49th Street) next door to the hotel. It is home to the Actor's Chapel. Inside is a shrine with statues of patron saints of the arts.

[18] Longacre Theatre

220 West 48th Street. Opened 1913.

After visiting the Longacre many times as a critic, Dorothy would make one more journey here in 1953 for her last effort as a playwright. She cowrote *The Ladies of the Corridor* with Arnaud d'Usseau, a playwright with a few modest successes under his belt, whom she had met at a cocktail party. The concept and setting—a group of lonely elderly women living out their remaining days together in a Manhattan residential hotel—were taken straight from her own life. One of the central characters, Lulu Ames, was a dead ringer for Hazel Morse, the boozy protagonist of Parker's most famous short story, "Big

86 | Dorothy Parker's New York

Blonde." To ensure that she would finish the play, d'Usseau kept Dorothy away from the bottle and enforced a strict work ethic.

The Ladies had tryout runs in Boston and Philadelphia then moved to New York in the fall. Among the cast were Edna Best, Vera Allen, Frances Starr, and a thirty-three-year-old Walter Matthau. On October 21, 1953, it opened to mixed reviews. Syndicated critic George Jean Nathan proclaimed it the best play of the year. But John Chapman of the *New York Daily News* had a less enthusiastic response: "The hazard inherent in the slice-of-life technique of play writing is that the slices may turn out to be just so much salami—and this is what happened to *The Ladies of the Corridor*." Another perspective was provided in the *Times* review by Brooks Atkinson: "The authors are entitled to credit for having written parts that can be acted so well."

The show couldn't make it through the holidays. It ran forty-five performances and closed November 28. Nonetheless, afterward Parker proclaimed *The Ladies of the Corridor* the work she was most proud of. In 2003 and 2005 the Peccadillo Theatre Co. dusted the play off for a highly successful off-Broadway run that was much more successful than its 1953 debut. Critic Honor Moore, writing in the *Times*, called the play "as unyielding and coruscating a portrait of women before feminism as I have ever seen." The attention prompted Penguin Classics to reissue the play in 2008 with a new introduction by Marion Meade. "It's the best play she wrote," Meade penned. "She always used to say, 'Well, I'm a feminist, I'm a feminist,' but she didn't act like a feminist, that's for sure. But in this play she proved, in fact, she was a feminist."

The Longacre was built in 1913 by Harry H. Frazee, who owned the Boston Red Sox and sold Babe Ruth to the New York Yankees.

Musicals were the bread and butter at the Longacre until it fell on hard times during the Depression; it ceased operation during World War II. From 1944 to 1953 it was leased for radio and TV shows; *The Ladies of the Corridor* was the first theatrical show in nine years. The Shubert Organization undertook a multimillion-dollar restoration in 2007 to 2008 that rehabilitated the French neoclassical facade and beaux arts interior while improving the sight lines and adding amenities for theatergoers.

[19] Guild/August Wilson Theatre

243–59 West 52nd Street. Opened 1925.

The Theatre Guild, a group founded in 1918 to put on high-quality, noncommercial plays, commissioned this building in the 1920s for the express purpose of being a theater showcase and a theatrical resource center. Fifteenth-century Tuscan villas inspired the facade. In March 1931 Dorothy was here to review George Bernard Shaw's *Getting Married*, starring the celebrity screen star Dorothy Gish, for *The New Yorker*. "I regret to say that during the first act of this, I, for what I hope will be my only time in the theater, fell so soundly asleep that the gentleman who brought me piled up a barricade of overcoat, hat, stick, and gloves between us to establish a separation in the eyes of the world, and went into an impersonation of A Young Man Who Has Come to the Theater Unaccompanied."

This 1925 theater seats about 1,200. It has changed hands many times and has had six different names. In 2005 it was named in honor of playwright August Wilson, a two-time Pulitzer Prize winner.

[20] Punch and Judy Theatre

55 West 49th Street. Opened 1914; demolished 1987.

After *No Sirree!* George S. Kaufman and Marc Connelly set to work on an even more elaborate production, a nonsequential revue. This time, however, the Algonquin regulars weren't in it; they hired professional actors and singers to play their parts. The show was called *The Forty-Niners*, in honor of their previous production. Opening on November 6, 1922, the show boasted original skits by Ring Lardner, Kaufman, and Connelly and a one-act historical drama called *Nero* by the team of Parker and Benchley. Unfortunately, no copies of the script remain. Despite Connelly's best efforts as the show's emcee, it ran for only fifteen performances. This would be the last time the Vicious Circle collaborated on anything.

Dorothy also visited this theater in March 1931—after it had become the Charles Hopkins—to review a play by A. A. Milne for *The New Yorker*, an assignment that probably did not thrill her. She had already panned *Winnie-the-Pooh* in *The New Yorker*, and Milne's latest play, *Give Me Yesterday*, fared no better with her:

> My dearest dread is the word "yesterday" in the name of a play; for I know that sometime during the evening I am going to be transported, albeit kicking and screaming, back to the scenes and the costumes of a tenderer time. And I know, who shows these scars to you, what the writing and the acting of those episodes of tenderer times are going to be like. I was not wrong, heaven help me, in my prevision of the Milne work. Its hero is caused, by novel device, to fall asleep and a-dream . . . and thus he is given yesterday. Me, I should have given him twenty years to life.

The theater opened as the Punch and Judy in 1914 and remained in operation until 1925. In 1926 it became the Charles Hopkins Theatre, named for the actor, who needed a place to try out experimental theater. It remained in business for only seven more years before becoming a movie house during the Depression. Later it showed X-rated movies until it was torn down in 1987 and replaced by an office tower.

[21] Lexington Theatre

569 Lexington Avenue. Opened 1914; demolished 1959.

In the summer of 1919, labor unrest swept Broadway, and the actors took part in strike benefits held in theaters around the city. This was before performers had union representation, and they were demanding better wages and benefits from the powerful producers who controlled the stage.

While covering the theater scene for *Vanity Fair*, Dorothy was invited to a benefit production put on by the Actors' Equity Association at the old Lexington Avenue Opera House, also known as the Lexington Theatre. It was an all-star evening, which she told readers about in the October 1919 issue:

> You can stand out in the lobby and be jostled by actors and actresses just as if you were one of them. You can buy a program—and get your change back—from one of a large flock of imminent ingénues. It is, undoubtedly, an evening to send night letters to the dear ones about. Marie Dresser, Eddie Cantor, W. C. Fields, Ivy Sawyer . . . you can see for yourself it is considerable entertainment . . . the big event of the bill was, of course, the second act of *The Lady of the Camellias*, done by Ethel and Lionel Barrymore . . . the Barrymores can never fail to be the big event of any bill on which they appear.

The Lexington Theatre was opened by Oscar Hammerstein (father of the noted lyricist) in 1914. His Lexington Avenue Opera House was the home for plays, musicals, movies, and vaudeville. The beautiful beaux arts theater had more than three thousand seats and three balconies. The building was sold to Marcus Loew, who converted it to a movie house for his chain. For more than fifty years it was the Loews Lexington movie theater. In 1955, Marilyn Monroe filmed the legendary "blowing white dress" scene for *The Seven Year Itch* by the theater. The building was demolished in 1959; in 1961 Judy Garland helped unveil the exceptionally bland-looking Summit Hotel where the theater once stood. It was the DoubleTree Metropolitan until the COVID-19 pandemic shuttered it.

Figure 33. A few minutes after this photo was taken, Dorothy Parker was arrested outside the Boston Statehouse. She was protesting the planned execution of accused anarchists Sacco and Vanzetti. *Source:* Dorothy Parker Society Archives.

5

Fighting for the Underdog
Activist

Many know Dorothy Parker as a gifted writer, but far fewer know of her staunch support for progressive social causes, from labor unions and civil rights to the Spanish resistance. Contrary and antiestablishment to the core, she was outraged by the powerful who took advantage of the weak. "A good many people, in my time, have called me stubborn" began one of the many political fundraising letters sent out with her signature during her lifetime. During the Cold War era, they called her worse than that: she was accused of being a Communist and was ultimately blacklisted, along with some three hundred of her peers, in the entertainment industry.

Dorothy's first public political statement came in 1927, when she was arrested during a march in Boston, fined, and released. She had traveled there to protest the planned execution of accused anarchists Nicola Sacco and Bartolomeo Vanzetti, a case that had become an international cause célèbre. George Bernard Shaw, H. G. Wells, and Edna St. Vincent Millay were among the many cultural figures of the day who had pronounced the trial a miscarriage of justice. Some Round Table members, including Robert Benchley, Heywood Broun, and Ruth Hale, lent various forms of support, but others "thought we were fools," Dorothy told an interviewer later. "They just didn't think about anything but the theater." Beginning in the mid-1930s, she involved herself in a sometimes-dizzying array of organizations, committees, and speaking engagements.

This work took time and energy that she could have devoted to her writing, but it may have fulfilled other needs. Like the Round Table in the 1920s, political involvement may have given her a sense of belonging, excitement, and importance—as well as genuine satisfaction, which she did not often get from the work that occupied most of her time, writing film scripts for Hollywood.

Membership Dossier

The Federal Bureau of Investigation compiled copious notes about Dorothy Parker's activities before, during, and after World War II. Often, it looks as if the agents got their leads from the newspapers, which reported almost everything she said. According to her FBI file, she had an extensive list of sponsorships, memberships, and official positions. Almost sixty years after her death, many pages of Parker's file remain redacted by the United States Department of Justice.

- Abraham Lincoln Brigade; sponsor

- American Committee for Protection of Foreign Born; sponsor

- American Committee for Yugoslav Relief; sponsor

- American Council for a Democratic Greece; member of the national board

- American Council on Soviet Relations; supporter

- American Relief Ship for Spain; sponsor

- American Slav Congress; sponsor

- American Youth for Democracy; toastmaster at annual dinner

- Artists Front to Win the War; sponsor

- Citizens Committee for Harry Bridges; sponsor

- Civil Rights Congress; signed petition

- Hollywood Anti-Nazi League; executive board member

- Hollywood League for Democratic Action; board member

- Joint Anti-Fascist Refugee Committee; acting chair

- League of American Writers; contributor

- League for Women Shoppers; national board member

- Medical Bureau to Aid Spanish Democracy; sponsor

- Motion Picture Artists Committee; executive board member

- National Citizens Political Action Committee; vice chair

- National Committee to Win the Peace; member

- National Council of American-Soviet Friendship; supporter

- New York Tom Mooney Committee; sponsor

- Southern Conference for Human Welfare; honorary member

- Spanish Children's Milk Fund; sponsor

- Spanish Refugee Appeal; chair

- United American Spanish Aid Committee; sponsor

From the Algonquin to Activism

Growing up in the upper middle class on the West Side of Manhattan, as a child Dorothy was witness to—although not a part of—the city breadlines. In a 1939 recollection written for the leftist *New Masses*, she speaks of how her awareness of inequality began during a childhood snowstorm on the Upper West Side:

> I was in a brownstone in New York, and there was a blizzard, and my rich aunt—a horrible woman then and now—had come to visit. I remember going to the window and seeing the street with the men shoveling snow; their hands were purple on the shovels, and their feet were wrapped with burlap. And my aunt, looking over my shoulder, said "Now isn't it nice there's a blizzard. All those men have work." And I knew then that it was not nice that men could work for their lives only in desperate weather, that there was no work for them when it was fair.[1]

During her youth and young adulthood, Dorothy's focus had been on socializing and writing. The end of the 1920s brought the demise of the Algonquin Round Table—which nobody seemed to notice at the time—as well as the O. Henry Award for her brilliant short story "Big Blonde" (1929). Soon thereafter, her first collection of short fiction, *Laments for the Living* (1930), and her third and final collection of light verse, *Death and Taxes* (1931), were published.

From 1929 to 1930 Dorothy spent more than a year in Europe, primarily Switzerland, living with her friends Gerald and Sara Murphy. After the couple's young son, Patrick, was diagnosed with tuberculosis, Sara asked Dorothy to join them in the Swiss resort town of Montana-Vermala while Patrick underwent treatment. After returning to New York in 1930 via luxury ocean liner, she lived in furnished apartments and hotel rooms in Manhattan.

In 1933 Dorothy met Alan Campbell, an actor and writer eleven years her junior. Her relationship with Alan changed the course of not only her personal but also her professional life. The couple, who married in 1934, moved to California and started writing screenplays. They made an effective team, with Alan blocking out scenes and Dorothy adding snappy dialogue.

Although many of the films were forgettable, the couple received an Academy Award nomination in 1937 for their work on *A Star Is Born*, and Dorothy was nominated again in 1947 for cowriting *Smash-Up: The Story of a Woman* with Frank Cavett. Legend has it she was an uncredited script doctor on the perennial holiday favorite *It's a Wonderful Life*. Despite these apparent successes, Dorothy disliked screenwriting and often spoke harshly of Hollywood, once describing it as "this lotus-laden shore / This Isle of Do-What's-Done-Before."

In her new life, Dorothy gave up many of the habits that had made her famous, trading long nights at speakeasies for long days in studio writers' buildings. She no longer wrote any light verse, nor did she review books or plays. Seeking "roots," she and Alan purchased a dilapidated farmhouse on 111 acres in Bucks County, Pennsylvania. They divided their time between the farmhouse and Los Angeles, with occasional visits to New York.

Over the next fifteen years Dorothy was a study in contrasts, earning $2,000 a week (around $45,000 today) as a screenwriter while crusading for the poor and oppressed. After discovering with dismay that the average screenwriter without a famous name made just $40 a week, she poured her energy into a several-year effort to build a union—the Screen Writers Guild—powerful enough to negotiate contracts with the studios. And her 1937 visit to civil war-racked Spain prompted a new round of activism.

Dorothy stayed friendly with only a few of her Round Table chums, including Robert Benchley, Marc Connelly, and Alexander Woollcott; others, such as Edna Ferber, George S. Kaufman, and Neysa McMein, she dropped completely. Some of her old pals thought she had grown tiresome because she was constantly talking politics. For her part, she preferred the company of those who shared her new passions.

During World War II, with Alan serving in Europe as an Army Air Forces officer, Dorothy moved into an apartment in New York and occupied much of her time with political and patriotic work. She even toured schools with poet Ogden Nash to promote

Figure 34. A December 1937 fundraiser featured Dorothy and Ambassador Fernando de Los Rios, the Spanish Republic representative to the United States, at the Hotel New Yorker (481 Eighth Avenue). After her visit to Spain that year, Parker served as chair of the women's division of the North American Committee to Aid Spanish Democracy, one of the many causes that she supported. *Source:* Dorothy Parker Society Archives.

the purchase of war bonds. Her older writing was repackaged and reprinted, paperbacks were issued of her collected poetry, and the first *Portable* edition appeared. Military personnel could read her short stories in a special armed forces edition sent to troops around the world.

The 1950s began on a positive note, however. Dorothy and Alan reconciled, and she moved back to Los Angeles with him. Their second marriage began on August 17, 1950; fifty-six-year-old Dorothy remarked to the press, "People who haven't talked to each other in years are on speaking terms again today—including the bride and groom."[2]

Fighting for the Underdog | 95

Figure 35. Map of Manhattan showing locations where Parker's political activity took place. *Source:* Collection of the author.

Parker and the Waiters' Strike

In February 1934 Dorothy was dating Alan, who, perhaps with her help, had just been cast in her friend Philip Barry's new play *The Joyous Season*.[3] One day she received a telephone call from Woollcott, one of her best friends, who wanted her support—for a strike. He called Benchley as well. The three founding members of the Vicious Circle, known primarily for their quick wit and one-liners, were starting to "get ink" for their roles as labor activists. This was a role well-suited to Dorothy, and she accepted the challenge readily; however, the night didn't go quite as planned.

The waiters at the **[1] Waldorf-Astoria Hotel, 301 Park Avenue**, were on strike. Two staff members from *Common Sense* magazine planned to cause a scene by standing

Figure 36. The grand Waldorf-Astoria Hotel lobby clock, made for the 1893 World's Columbian Exposition in Chicago, was loaned to the New-York Historical Society while the hotel was renovated. *Source:* Photo by the author.

up during a dinner in the blue and gold Empire Room when the orchestra took a break. They would read a statement and urge all the patrons in the room to march out in support of the waiters picketing outside.

The mission of the three Round Tablers was to pretend to be diners and, at the right moment, march out with those supporting the strike. The magazine activists had foolishly tipped off the press and management that a demonstration was to take place, however, so the dining room was loaded with reporters and hotel detectives.

The trio bundled into fur coats and headed over to the hotel. They took a table and waited for the action. At 8 p.m. two activists jumped up and started reading their speech urging a walkout. Detectives jumped on the pair and began to beat them up. As the *Times* reported, tables were overturned and fists flew.

Parker, Benchley, and Woollcott stood up and started shouting insults and wisecracks as the men fought. Dorothy asked if it was a private fight, or "could anyone get in on it?" As the demonstrators were hauled out, the newspaper reported that the trio "gibed at the detectives with a running fire of extemporaneous bon mots and 'wisecracks' as Selden Rodman [an organizer] and his friend were mauled. They escaped unscathed."

Spanish Refugee Appeal

Considerably less lighthearted was Dorothy's work with the Spanish Refugee Appeal of the Joint Anti-Fascist Refugee Committee, an organization she supported for years. The group's offices were in a nondescript building in Chelsea at **[2] 23 West 26th Street**.

In 1937, after she had moved to Hollywood, Dorothy traveled with Alan to Europe, where they spent time in Madrid and Valencia. Spain was then in the middle of a civil war, in which leftist forces were battling Francisco Franco, the fascist leader supported by Hitler and Mussolini. Deeply shaken by the suffering she saw, Dorothy redoubled her efforts to help the anti-Franco cause upon her return to the United States.

She enthusiastically lent her name to the Spanish Refugee Appeal, which sent out countless fundraising letters bearing her signature. As with the Sacco and Vanzetti case, she was in good company; cultural figures of the day were flocking to the cause. The organization's pamphlet *Spain and Peace* had a cover by Pablo Picasso and text by Howard Fast, who would later write *Spartacus*.

Dorothy's literary output was also affected by her experience in Spain. Upon her return she wrote the touching and strikingly Hemingwayesque "Soldiers of the Republic," which *The New Yorker* published in February 1938. One of her most mature short stories, it describes an evening in a Valencian café with a group of Spanish soldiers who pay for drinks after the narrator gives them cigarettes. This story has some wonderfully subtle touches of narrative detail: "It was dark outside, the quick, new dark that leaps down without dusk on the day; but, because there were no lights in the streets, it seemed as set and as old as midnight. So you wondered that all the babies were still up. There were babies everywhere in the café, babies serious without solemnity and interested in a tolerant way in their surroundings." The story revolves around the narrator's sense of delicate self-awareness and her characteristic dash of irony: "Darling of me to share my cigarettes with the men on their way back to the trenches. Little Lady Bountiful. The prize sow."

World War II Digs

After their European trip, Dorothy and Alan returned to screenwriting, political work, and refurbishing their farmhouse. During World War II, with Alan away in uniform,

Figure 37. The Commodore Hotel, with Pershing Square in the foreground, around 1919. The hotel is still present; today, it is covered in steel and glass from a 1970s gut renovation. *Source:* Irving Underhill, Library of Congress, Prints and Photographs Division.

Fighting for the Underdog | 99

Dorothy continued spending time in Hollywood but also decided to reestablish a New York residence. She chose a two-room apartment at the **[3] New Weston Hotel, 31 West 49th Street**, a twelve-story luxury hotel that had opened in 1906. It was designed with Old World élan: all the interiors were of mahogany and the furniture was custom made. In the 1930s the Basque government used the New Weston as home after fleeing the civil war in Spain. Later, the hotel was popular with British tourists and business travelers who enjoyed the afternoon tea service in the lobby. The hotel was demolished in 1966; the following year, a forty-story office building called 437 Madison was erected in its place.

The New Weston was not far from the center of Dorothy's old life, the Algonquin Hotel. More important for her new life, it was close to venues such as the Commodore Hotel, which hosted many of the political events and fundraisers that increasingly filled her time.

Today's Guest Speaker is Dorothy Parker

Throughout the 1940s Dorothy was a popular guest speaker and host for political events and fundraisers, many of which were held at the **[4] Commodore Hotel, 125 East 42nd Street** (at Lexington Avenue). Located smack in the middle of Manhattan and adjacent to Grand Central Terminal, the Commodore (renamed the Grand Hyatt in 1980) was for decades the most popular New York location for large-scale events.

A sampling of Dorothy's visits here demonstrates the range of her political involvements. In March 1939, she was one of several foreign correspondents and writers addressing a meeting of the Medical Bureau and the North American Committee to Aid Spanish Democracy, groups that were raising funds for refugees of the civil war. In December 1943 she attended a fundraiser for the Joint Anti-Fascist Refugee Committee honoring Lillian Hellman. In January 1945 she addressed a luncheon for the same committee, applauding attendees for aiding those suffering under Franco. And in March 1945 she chaired a luncheon at the Commodore honoring First Lady Eleanor Roosevelt, sponsored by the Southern Conference for Human Welfare, an interracial coalition of Southern progressives founded in 1938.

Designed by architects Whitney Warren and Charles D. Wetmore, who also planned Grand Central Terminal, completed in 1919, the Commodore was named after Cornelius "Commodore" Vanderbilt, who built the first Grand Central. It offered 1,956 guest rooms on twenty-eight floors, making it one of the largest hotels in the city. The Commodore claimed to have the largest banquet and ballroom in North America—it could seat 3,500 for dinner—and hosted many of the nation's most distinguished functions. Its

100 | Dorothy Parker's New York

large ballroom and proximity to the train station made it perfect for public events held by political groups.

The Commodore has a rich history of famous visitors. Scott and Zelda Fitzgerald moved to the hotel during their honeymoon in April 1920 after being thrown out of the nearby Biltmore. When they arrived, they pushed themselves around the revolving doors for half an hour. President Franklin Roosevelt watched his election returns here, and it was here in 1948 that Richard Nixon, heading a subcommittee of the House Un-American Activities Committee, confronted accused spy Alger Hiss with his accuser, Whittaker Chambers. Before it was renovated, the hotel also had the grim distinction of being one of the most popular locations in the city for people to leap to their death.

An early Donald Trump deal transformed the Commodore into a splashy 1,400-room upscale hotel in the late 1970s. The old hotel was completely gutted, and a massive glass curtain was bolted to its exterior, sheathing it in a wall of glass. In 1980 it reopened as the New York Grand Hyatt Hotel.

A Hall for the People

Dorothy was involved in at least one event at [5] **Town Hall, 123 West 43rd Street**: a talk by novelist Josephine Herbst about her experiences in Spain. The event was part of a luncheon for the Women's Committee of the Medical Bureau to Aid Spanish Democracy, of which Dorothy was a sponsor. But given Dorothy's interest in politics, she may well have visited Town Hall regularly. Long a champion of free speech, this vibrant institution has hosted thousands of lectures, concerts, plays, and other events in its many decades of existence.

Town Hall was the brainchild of suffragists who wanted a meeting space where people could be educated on the important issues of the day. In keeping with their democratic principles, the auditorium was designed so that all seats would be roughly equal: it has no box or obstructed-view seats. While the finishing touches were being put to the building, the Nineteenth Amendment was passed, giving women the right to vote, so the suffragists had two reasons to celebrate when the hall opened on January 12, 1921.

Since opening, Town Hall has played an important role in the political and cultural life of the city. In its founding year, birth control advocate Margaret Sanger was arrested while she was onstage; in 1929 a commemoration of the second anniversary of the execution of Sacco and Vanzetti was held here, after officials in Boston denied the use of Faneuil Hall for the event. Town Hall hosted poet Edna St. Vincent Millay's first public reading and contralto Marian Anderson's New York debut. Today, the hall is a venue for comedians, jazz concerts, film seminars, and cultural lectures. The interior of this National Historic Landmark is adorned with framed programs from some of these events and many more.

Seeing Red

Many of the organizations Dorothy worked with in the 1940s came to be considered Communist fronts by the FBI. As anti-Communism began to sweep the country following World War II, Parker and her friends on the left found themselves attacked as "un-American." The FBI investigated them, and government panels demanded that they renounce their beliefs and inform on others. Many were ultimately blacklisted, and some were even imprisoned or fled the country.

In January 1941 Whittaker Chambers, a former member of the Communist Party turned anti-Communist, published a scathing article in *Time* called "The Revolt of the Intellectuals," which attacked Dorothy, Malcolm Cowley (an editor and friend of Parker), John Steinbeck, Lillian Hellman, and other "literary liberals." Chambers charged that during the Depression such intellectuals had decided that socialism was the way to cure the severe economic problems in the United States; some, he said, had even traveled to the USSR to embrace the Soviets and Stalin. Chambers viewed Dorothy as an ally of the Communists, though not a Communist herself.

When the U.S. government started seeking out "Reds" after the war, the people mentioned in Chambers's article were some of the first to be scrutinized. In 1947 the House Un-American Activities Committee turned its attentions to Hollywood and began subpoenaing actors, writers, and directors it suspected of Communist sympathies. Although she was not called before the committee, Dorothy publicly denounced the effort from the beginning. The Department of Justice maintains the files of the FBI. The dossier on Dorothy Parker is more than an inch thick.

Red Scare in Times Square

Yet another hotspot for political activity was the **[6] Hotel Astor, 1515 Broadway**, between 44th and 45th streets. In late 1945, during National Children's Book Week, a luncheon was held at the Hotel Astor, attended by seven hundred writers, editors, parents, librarians, and teachers. The theme was "One World" and the aim was to improve U.S.-Soviet ties.

The FBI was investigating the American Council on Soviet Relations and the National Council of American-Soviet Friendship, to which Dorothy was lending her name. Thus, she ended up in their files once again. FBI special agents attending the luncheon

102 | Dorothy Parker's New York

Figure 38. The Hotel Astor was a popular destination for decades. It had a rooftop bar and restaurant (which could seat five hundred) that was legendary and immortalized by Cole Porter. *Source:* George Grantham Bain Collection, Library of Congress, Prints and Photographs Division.

reported, "She said that according to Hearst and Patterson Press the next war would be between the United States and Russia; we hold out our hands to our friends, our allies, our sisters and brothers, the people of the Soviet Union. There is no better way to reach the people of the Soviet Union than by books." Dorothy then introduced Mrs. Eugene D. Kisselev, wife of the Soviet consul general in New York City, and presented her with a package of books that had been chosen by American children. Parker was back for another dinner, this time to mark the tenth anniversary of the Veterans of the Abraham Lincoln Brigade, on February 12, 1947. The dinner honored the American volunteers who had fought against Franco.

For more than sixty years, the Astor was one of the most famous hotels in the city, located on the west side of Broadway. The hotel's builders had staked a claim to this part of town before the theaters arrived, when it was still the city's edge and a row of brownstone homes marked the residential neighborhood. The Astor and the subway both opened in 1904. The hotel had a famous roof garden and dining room, the largest in

New York. But the last guest checked out in 1967, and the building was then demolished. A fifty-four-story building called One Astor Plaza (1515 Broadway) was constructed in its place; today, it is the home of MTV and Nickelodeon.

The FBI opened a file on Dorothy that ultimately grew to three hundred pages, although much of the now-released material is hardly damning: Howard Fast's twenty-page *Spain and Peace* pamphlet; a letter from a high school student researching a term paper; and Dorothy's own fundraising letters for various causes, helpfully forwarded to the FBI by gossip columnist Walter Winchell. But decades after Parker's death, the government still keeps numerous sections of her file redacted for "national security" reasons. According to her FBI file, from 1939 to 1950 Parker was associated with thirty-three organizations that the agency considered Communist fronts. FBI agents grilled her in an April 1951 visit to her Los Angeles home. They reported that she had a "neat appearance" but "appeared to be a nervous type person."

In 1950 the anti-Communist newsletter *Counterattack* included Dorothy's name in its publication *Red Channels*, a report listing 151 directors, performers, and writers with alleged Communist sympathies. Ironically, the report was published from [7] **55 West 42nd Street**, a non-descript office building (since demolished) that was home to many publishers and international missions to the United Nations. Compiled from a variety of sources, *Red Channels* was one of the documents on which the Hollywood blacklist was based.

Ultimately, some 320 people—including Dorothy—were blacklisted and barred from working in Hollywood because of their alleged Communist ties. The blacklist made obtaining work difficult, and it also contributed to the failure of Dorothy's second marriage. As the government investigations increased, Alan, a veteran, became terrified that he would be blacklisted by association with Dorothy. They separated again after scarcely more than a year together since he returned from World War II.

Publicly, though, Parker seemed unfazed by the government's unwelcome attentions. She certainly did not stop her political activities. In a 1952 speech in New York as chair of the Spanish Refugee Appeal, Dorothy, wearing sunglasses, said she wasn't hiding her identity from the FBI, for whom she "had only monumental scorn." The sunglasses, she told the crowd of 450, were "to cover a nasty infected eye probably from watching these [presidential] conventions over television." After reading a letter from Irish playwright Seán O'Casey supporting Spain, she raised her clenched fist in the Popular Front salute and gave a cry of "Salude!" At a rally in New York the following year, she was again defiant: "It's a short step from being told what to think to being told not to think at all."[4]

In January 1955, a few years after Dorothy was interviewed by the FBI in Los Angeles, agents came knocking again, this time at the [8] **Hotel Volney, 23 East 74th**

Street. In his "Lyons Den" column that March, *New York Post* columnist Leonard Lyons wrote: "Two government men came to the apartment of Dorothy Parker. They wanted to question her about some of her left-wing committee affiliations. Parker's two pet dogs romped all over the room, paying no heed to her command to stay put. When the questioners asked about the extent of her influence upon the committees, Parker replied: "My influence? Look at these two dogs of mine. I can't even influence them.""

Black and White

Long before she decided to leave her literary estate to Martin Luther King Jr., Dorothy was sensitive to racial injustice. Her landmark short story for *The New Yorker*, "Arrangement in Black and White," written in 1927, took aim at white prejudice and hypocrisy; the story was based on an evening with the internationally renowned singer Paul Robeson, a longtime friend whom she greatly admired. In the mid-1930s she helped raise funds for the defense of the Scottsboro Boys, nine Black teenagers sentenced to death for allegedly raping two white women in Alabama. What disturbed her most about America, she told an interviewer, was injustice, intolerance, stupidity, and segregation—particularly segregation.

Two decades later, she rose to Robeson's defense when he became the first American to be banned from television. In March 1950, NBC canceled his scheduled appearance on *Today* with Eleanor Roosevelt. Dorothy immediately sent a telegram to NBC president Sidney Eiges in protest.

Robeson had made frequent trips to the Soviet Union and had asserted that he felt freer there, as a Black person, than in the United States. In the Cold War era, such statements ignited a firestorm of controversy. The U.S. government declared him a Communist and blacklisted him. Several months later, it revoked his passport; now he could neither make a living in the United States (because of the blacklist) nor travel abroad to give concerts. To satisfy requests for concerts outside U.S. borders, he resorted to singing over long-distance telephone lines.

In the ensuing years, his supporters would stage numerous benefits for him, including a dinner on October 14, 1954, at the **[9] Manhattan Towers Hotel, 2162 Broadway**, at which Dorothy spoke. Other tribute speeches were given by W. E. B. DuBois, editor in chief of *Crisis* magazine; Rockwell Kent, American painter and printmaker; and screenwriter Ring Lardner Jr. The FBI had an informant there who ignored the content of the speeches but noted in Parker's file that dinner cost $7.50 a plate. Today, a different type of sweating takes place; the basement auditorium was converted to a fitness club in 2010.

Fighting for the Underdog | 105

Dorothy Takes the Fifth

A courtroom might seem the least likely place to spot Dorothy Parker, and it was the one destination where her beloved poodle could not accompany her. But on a winter's day in February 1955, at the height of the Cold War, she was summoned to a legislative hearing in room 408 of the **[10] Supreme Court of the State of New York, 60 Centre Street**. Inside this imposing classical-style landmark, its entrance marked by ten massive granite columns, Dorothy invoked the Fifth Amendment (protection against self-incrimination) when asked if she was a Communist.

In the front of the building are the engraved words of George Washington: "The true administration of justice is the firmest pillar of good government." On this particular day, a government panel with an extremely long name—the New York State Joint Legislative Committee on Charitable and Philanthropic Agencies and Organizations—was conducting an investigation of the alleged diversion of $3.5 million in charitable contributions to Communist organizations. It had called Parker to testify because one target of its investigation was the Joint Anti-Fascist Refugee Committee, which the U.S. government had declared a Communist front.

Parker—who "wore a mink jacket and oversized cocoa-colored Tyrolean hat," the *New York World-Telegram* dutifully reported—insisted she had not known that the committee was controlled by the Communist Party. She had been the national chair of the organization, she said, which was why all the fundraising letters sent out from 23 West 26th had carried her signature. But she had not composed the letters herself, nor had she asked how the organization spent the funds raised: "My job was to raise money and that's all."[5]

Shortly after this hearing, the FBI closed its investigation of Parker, concluding that she was not dangerous enough to include in its "Security Index." By then, however, the damage to her career, life, and spirit had already been done, and the echoes would reverberate in the future. In 1958, for instance, after *Esquire* began publishing her book reviews, the magazine received angry letters from readers: Why were they employing a Communist?

Purpose over Poetry

By the 1950s, Dorothy's inclination to write the short social satires and clever poetry of her earlier, more carefree days had essentially vanished, along with her former way of life. It was in politics that the ever-battling Parker found a new use for her wit and insight.

As she entered her sixties, though, Dorothy found herself with more limited avenues for creative expression. Her newer writing, reflecting her more mature concerns, was often thought too serious or polemical. Some editors—such as Harold Ross—wanted her to write as she once had, but she now felt that "there are things that never have been funny, and never will be." The blacklist had closed some doors, and the demise of Hollywood's golden age had closed others, making the task of obtaining and completing work more challenging.

And so, the New York life she would return to in her final years was quieter than that of her younger days. In some ways she would garner even more respect and recognition than in her heyday, but at the same time she would continue to face the same demon she always had: loneliness.

Figure 39. On her seventieth birthday in 1963, Dorothy Parker was surrounded by review copies mailed to her West Hollywood home for the *Esquire* column. *Source:* Dorothy Parker Society Archives.

6

If You Can Get through the Twilight, You'll Live through the Night

The 1950s and 1960s were unkind to Dorothy Parker. She contributed infrequent book reviews to *Esquire*, her final Broadway play flopped, and she faced repeated government questions about her left-wing activities. During the gloomy Eisenhower era, when her lonely life in Manhattan had become unbearable, she gave up her apartment in the Volney Hotel and moved back to Los Angeles to rejoin Alan for a few more years. The reunited pair lived in a bungalow Alan had purchased in West Hollywood. But in June 1963, she discovered Alan's body after his apparent suicide by overdosing on alcohol and barbiturates.[1] Dorothy decided to move back to Manhattan for good.

Now seventy years old, she was happy to return to her favorite city. "You just don't know how I love it—how I get up every morning and want to kiss the pavement . . . Hollywood smells like a laundry," she told Ward Morehouse of the *The New York World-Telegram and The Sun*. "The beautiful vegetables taste as if they were raised in trunks, and at those wonderful supermarkets you find that the vegetables are all wax. The flowers out there smell like dirty, old dollar bills."

She spent her final years on the Upper East Side, befriended by socialite Gloria Vanderbilt and the actor Zero Mostel. She lived alone with her poodles, Misty and C'est Tout (That's All). Sometimes she needed an in-home health aide to help her care for herself. Dorothy had spills on sidewalks, her vision was poor, and her health was declining. Friends were few, but among the most devoted was Beatrice Ames Stewart, the first wife of Vicious Circle member Donald Ogden Stewart. Bea came over to cook for Dorothy or invited her to her apartment on the Upper East Side. When it was time to go, Bea had to give Dorothy pocket change for taxi fare.

Figure 40. Map of the Upper East Side featuring Parker's locations in her final years. *Source:* Collection of the author.

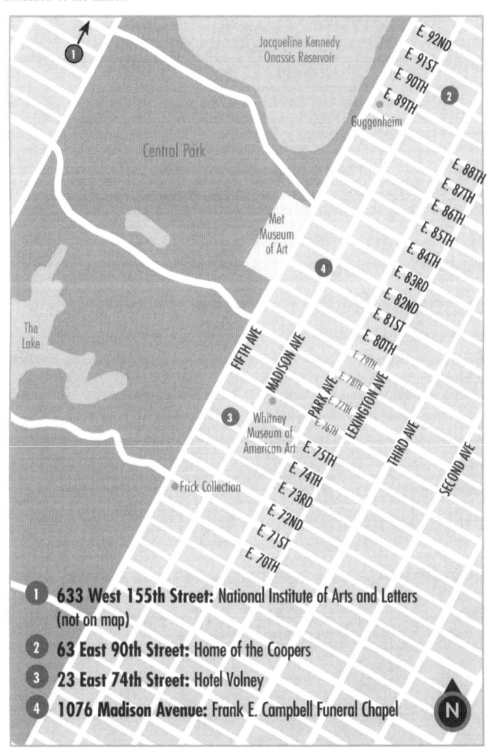

Sara Murphy, a widow now, also lived in the building. The old friends looked out for each other, just like it was 1929 on the Côte d'Azur. But most people forgot she was still around. When Truman Capote threw his famous Black and White Ball at the Plaza in November 1966, he claimed he had left Dorothy off the VIP guest list because he didn't know she was still alive.

Academic Recognition and Marilyn Monroe

When Dorothy was pushing sixty-five, her peers finally recognized her for her lifetime of work and achievements. In 1958 the [1] **National Institute of Arts and Letters, 633 West 155th Street** (by Trinity Cemetery), tapped Dorothy for the most prestigious literary award of her career: the Marjorie Peabody Waite Award, newly established to be given to a nonmember of the institute, "conferred annually on an older person" for her "lifelong achievement in literature." The ceremony was held at the institute on May 21, 1958.

Figure 41. The former home of Gloria Vanderbilt and Wyatt Cooper is around the corner from Park Avenue, Cooper Hewitt, and Central Park. *Source:* Photo by the author.

Dorothy went uptown to graciously accept. Editor and poet Malcolm Cowley, the president of the organization, read the tribute, written by Lillian Hellman: "To Dorothy Parker, born in West End, New Jersey, because the clean wit of her verse and the sharp perception in her stories has produced a brilliant record of our time. Because Miss Parker has a true talent, even her early work gives us as much pleasure today as it did thirty years ago."

Cowley was surprised that Dorothy was given a standing ovation, uncommon at the time. Dorothy went home on a cloud, with the prize and a thousand dollars in her purse. The following year she was elected a member of the National Institute of Arts and Letters. She showed up for the affair quite drunk, and her behavior was far from the standards of academic decorum usually observed at these events. She shared the stage with Arthur Miller, who was being honored with a drama prize. Dorothy seized the opportunity to meet the famous playwright—or, more precisely, his wife, Marilyn Monroe.

Under a Comfortable Wing

While living in Los Angeles and working as a screenwriting team, Dorothy and Alan had befriended a Southern actor-writer named Wyatt Cooper. The handsome young man was a close friend of the couple in 1961; the trio even cashed their unemployment checks together. In 1963 Cooper married Gloria Vanderbilt and relocated to New York, to **[2] 63 East 90th Street**. This was around the same time that Dorothy moved back to Manhattan after Alan's death.

The Coopers took Dorothy under their wing. They invited her to their stylish home for dinners and cocktail parties and included her in their rarefied circle of rich friends—a social scene Dorothy hadn't been part of since before World War II. They hosted parties with her as the guest of honor. She rubbed shoulders with CBS chairman Bill Paley and his glamorous wife, Babe; publisher Bennett Cerf; novelist Louis Auchincloss; journalist Gloria Steinem; lyricist Richard Adler; and many others.

She also became friendly with actor Zero Mostel, who had also been questioned by the government.

Cooper wrote the definitive story of Parker's later years for *Esquire* magazine. His article "Whatever You Think Dorothy Parker Was Like, She Wasn't" appeared in July 1968. It is the only first-person accounting of the last chapter in her life. One of the most poignant stories Cooper relates is that Dorothy didn't think she had the right clothes for 1960s Manhattan high society, so the Coopers outfitted her in the latest fashions. Over the years, Dorothy had lampooned dozens of high-society characters similar to Gloria Vanderbilt in her fiction, but ironically, as Dorothy approached the twilight of her life, the ultrarich Vanderbilt ended up being one of her most faithful friends.

In the winter of 1964 to 1965 Parker and Steinem sat down for an interview for *Ladies' Home Journal*. The pair hit it off; later they would go to movies and cultural events together. Steinem, a masterful storyteller, describes the day:

> Was she glad to be back in New York? "Oh my God *yes*," she said. "I looked forward to it every single day. California is nothing but money and what picture did you do, and Hollywood is a desert, a ghost town. Alan and I (her second husband, actor and playwright Alan Campbell) stayed there because of work—actually, I've lived there quite a lot and I hate it more each time. I stayed on after he died in order to close the house and take care of things." She sighed, and Troy crawled into her lap as if in sympathy. "New York is home, and I love everything about it, including the dirt. It does seem to me that people are a little more unfriendly and cross than I remember—they walk fast, but seem listless: strange—but perhaps I just anticipated too much and was bound to be disappointed. Still, New York is the only place to be in the whole country."

In March 1966, Parker gave her last recorded interview to New York radio station WBAI. Broadcaster Richard Lamparski asked Dorothy about specific stories and moments in her career. "I gave up writing verse shortly after you were born because I wasn't getting any better," she said. "This magnificent gesture went totally unnoticed, I may say."

Figure 42. During World War II, Dorothy Parker worked on screenplays and volunteered for the war effort. *Source:* Dorothy Parker Society Archives.

What the Hell? Words and Phrases Attributed to Parker

"What the hell" and "one night stand" are just two of the many phrases that Dorothy Parker is credited with popularizing, according to editor Stuart Y. Silverstein, who put together *Not Much Fun: The Lost Poems of Dorothy Parker* (1996). Spending hundreds of hours poring over vintage copies of magazines and newspapers, he managed to dig up more than one hundred pieces that Parker had written and, for whatever reason, neglected to publish in her three books of collected verse.

Silverstein says that Parker made numerous contributions to everyday speech. He also noted that "in virtually all instances the person credited with the first known use of a word or phrase almost certainly did not create it . . . Most words emerge from a hazy mist—suddenly, there they are, out of nowhere." According to Silverstein, the first documented use of the following words, terms, and phrases can be attributed to Dorothy Parker:

art moderne	one night stand
ball of fire	pain in the neck
with bells on	pass (sexual overture)
bellyacher	doesn't have a prayer
birdbrain	queer (gay)
boy-meets-girl	scaredy cat
daisy chain	the sky's the limit
face-lift	what the hell
high society	wisecrack
mess around	

Figure 43. The Volney is directly across Central Park from where Dorothy Parker grew up. *Source:* Photo by the author.

114 | Dorothy Parker's New York

One Last Residential Hotel

Dorothy Parker spent most of her life living in rented rooms. Fittingly, she died in one as well. The **[3] Volney at 23 East 74th Street**, an Upper East Side apartment house built in 1929, was a residential hotel just like all the others. At the end of her life, this was where Dorothy entertained a handful of friends and doted on her dogs. The hotel was filled with old women like her who owned dogs. She had a two-room apartment on the eighth floor in the twelve-story building.

Dorothy lived at the Volney twice. In the 1950s she rented a room when she was working on *The Ladies of the Corridor*. Once she finished the play, she moved back to Los Angeles to be with Alan. After Alan's death in 1963, she returned to the hotel for the last four years of her life. When Dorothy turned seventy, an interviewer asked what she was going to do next. She responded with her usual deadpan candor, "If I had any decency, I'd be dead. All my friends are."

But death waited until she was seventy-three, when it arrived in the form of a coronary on June 7, 1967. A housekeeper found her in bed. The hotel immediately called her friend Bea Stewart, who came to collect Dorothy's dog, Troy, and got in touch with Lillian Hellman. Hellman then notified the newspapers, and the next morning Dorothy's death made the front page of the *Times*, with an article that ran for most of another inside page. The article covered the highlights of her life and included kind appraisals of her oeuvre.

New Yorker editor William Shawn opined, "Miss Parker, along with Robert Benchley, E. B. White, James Thurber, Frank Sullivan, Ogden Nash, and Peter Arno, was one of the original group of contributors to *The New Yorker*, who, under Harold Ross's guidance, set the magazine's general tone and direction in its early years."[2]

Hellman had been among Dorothy's small circle of friends and one of the few people she trusted. After Alan died, Parker asked Hellman for help in managing her finances. Parker had owned a treasured Picasso, good enough to be shown in the Wildenstein Gallery, that she gave to Hellman to sell to cover medical bills. After Parker's body was removed from the Volney, Hellman dispatched workers to clean out the apartment.[3] No one knows what happened to Dorothy's personal papers, letters, mementos, clothes, and jewelry. Hellman died in 1984 without telling anyone what had become of her friend's possessions.

In many ways, Parker had come full circle. In an often-itinerant life that included homes in California, Pennsylvania, and even abroad, her last apartment was a twenty-minute walk across the park from her girlhood home. The Volney is in the Upper East Side Historic District, comprising the beaux arts–style town houses, penthouses, and private carriage houses erected for New York's wealthiest citizens in the early twentieth century. A two-bedroom apartment in the building sold for $2.2 million in 2024.

Figure 44. A send-off here, at Frank E. Campbell funeral chapel, is a symbol of status and success in New York. It was renovated after the COVID-19 pandemic and made even more grand. *Source:* Photo by the author.

Epitaph for a Darling Lady

Dorothy didn't want anyone to make a fuss or plan a funeral. But Hellman held one anyway at the [4] **Frank E. Campbell funeral chapel, 1076 Madison Avenue**, just seven blocks from the Volney. A crowd of about 150 attended the thirty-five minute ceremony. Hellman asked Zero Mostel to open for her. Mostel was in the middle of principle photography of *The Producers* and departed Mel Brooks's set for the morning to attend with his wife, Kate Mostel. She met Parker when she played Irma in *The Ladies of the Corridor* in 1953. The service began with a violinist performing Bach's immortal "Air on the G String." An overflow crowd spilled into the hallway.

Mostel told the gathering that Dorothy had not wanted a memorial: "If she had it her way, I suspect she would not be here at all." Hellman's eulogy recalled that her friend's famous wit "was that it stayed in no place, and was of no time." She said Dorothy was "until the very end, young and sparkling. . . . She was part of nothing and nobody except herself. . . . It was this independence of mind and spirit that was her true distinction." Hellman recalled for the mourners what Dorothy had observed: "It's not the tragedies that kill us, it's the messes." Old friend Sid Perelman had a lighter take on the proceedings: "I'm sure Dorothy's foot was tapping, even through as short an exercise as that, because she had a very short fuse."

In attendance were at least eight actresses: Frances Chaney, Madeline Lee Gilford, Nedda Harrigan Logan, Kate Mostel, Cathleen Nesbitt, Thelma Ritter, Maureen Stapleton, and fellow Algonquin Round Table member Peggy Wood.

Mourners included author Cleveland Amory, longtime friend George Oppenheimer, fellow blacklist actor Jack Gilford, *Esquire* publisher Arnold Gringrich, *New York Post* publisher Dorothy Schiff, and Thomas Guinzburg, representing Parker's publisher, Viking Press. Ring Lardner Jr., someone Dorothy knew as a teenager and later a blacklisted screenwriter, attended with his wife, Frances Chaney. Bea Stewart came to say goodbye, but her ex-husband, Don Stewart—the retired radical—was exiled in London. Gloria Vanderbilt had given birth on June 3 to a son, Anderson Hays Cooper, so she could not attend. Her husband, Wyatt Cooper, represented the family.

Frank E. Campbell's five-story building, built in 1910, is a New York institution. Campbell opened the business as the first "funeral church" in 1898. He revolutionized the upscale memorial service industry; prior to Campbell, many wealthy families held services in their homes. Famous send-offs at Campbell's include Roscoe "Fatty" Arbuckle, Jean-Michel Basquiat, Joan Crawford, Judy Garland, Texas Guinan, George S. Kaufman, John Lennon, and Biggie Smalls. In 2024 Campbell's completed a multi-million-dollar renovation and expansion, which added a 1,500-foot roof terrace for the bereaved to socialize outdoors.

Following the brief service, the body of Dorothy Parker, in a rented limousine and rental casket, was driven twenty miles north along the bucolic Saw Mill River Parkway to Hartsdale, Westchester County. This was the location of Ferncliff Cemetery and Mausoleum, the region's leader at the time in cremation services. However, rather than being the end of Parker's story, it was merely the quiet beginning of a whole new, bizarre final chapter.

7

Baltimore to the Bronx
The Epic Epilogue

Dorothy Parker's remains were taken to suburban Westchester County wearing a gold designer satin dress that was a gift from Gloria Vanderbilt Cooper. Her body arrived at the gates of Ferncliff Cemetery, **280 Secor Road, Hartsdale, New York**. Whether the cost of the cremation was part of the funeral services provided by Frank E. Campbell (a funeral billed to the estate at $634[1]) or not isn't known. What is a fact is that Ferncliff cremated Parker on June 9, 1967.

The following month, Parker's last will and testament was filed with the Surrogate Court in New York County. Parker owned no property and did not have a life insurance policy. She donated her literary estate to Dr. Martin Luther King Jr. She named the acerbic Lillian Hellman as her *executrix*, a term that has fallen out of fashion and is today the gender-neutral *executor*. An executor is usually paid a flat fee for the trouble. Within a year of Parker's death, Dr. King was assassinated, and the Parker bequest of $20,448.39 (about $190,000 today) went to the National Association for the Advancement of Colored People.[2] To this day, the NAACP benefits from the royalties on all Parker publications and her film, stage, and music productions.

Hellman was furious and took legal action, which was ultimately unsuccessful. All of Parker's belongings and papers vanished; if Hellman hired a cleanout service and junked it all is not clear. No Parker archive or letters were donated to any institution by Hellman. It is possible, but not proven, that everything was put on the curb on East 74th Street.

Hellman, who made all funeral arrangements, never told Ferncliff what to do with the ashes. Parker's cremains sat on a storeroom shelf in Hartsdale. The closest relatives

119

Figure 45. Ferncliff Cemetery is where Dorothy Parker's remains were cremated and stored. Among the cemetery's permanent residents are her friend Franklin P. Adams, James Baldwin, Moss Hart, and Toots Shor. *Source:* Photo by the author.

were her niece, Helen Droste Iveson, and nephew, George Henry Droste. In August 1967 they consented to the probate of the will. However, as Parker's only family, they were never consulted about anything related to their aunt's cremains or even queried whether their family—their Rothschild grandparents—had a cemetery plot somewhere.[3] They were left nothing. George, who died in 1977, and Helen, who died in 1988, never learned what became of their famous aunt.

Hellman, who would live until 1984, never replied to any inquiries from Ferncliff Cemetery about the cremation bill. Six years after Parker's death, on July 16, 1973, the ashes were boxed up and shipped to the thirtieth-floor law offices of O'Dwyer & Bernstien at **99 Wall Street**. The law firm had no idea what to do with the little can either. They did not contact the niece and nephew, though O'Dwyer & Bernstien had their home addresses and phone numbers in the office's files. In May 1974, Parker's attorney, Oscar Bernstien, died at eighty-nine. Paul O'Dwyer, at the time, was New York City Council president. With his law partner gone, O'Dwyer now held the cremains of one of their famous clients.

Figure 46. Attorney Paul O'Dwyer was born in County Mayo, Ireland. He was active in politics for decades and had scores of high-profile clients, from accused Communists to Irish Republican Army gunmen. *Source:* Bernard Gotfryd photograph collection, Library of Congress, Prints and Photographs Division.

From Broadway to Baltimore

For the next fifteen years, those few ounces of ash lived in a lawyer's filing cabinet. When Marion Meade was researching her Villard Books biography, *Dorothy Parker, What Fresh Hell is This?*, she visited O'Dwyer in his office. It was only then that he revealed to her that Parker's cremains were on the premises. Meade, who had flown to Syracuse, New York, to interview niece Helen Droste Iveson for her book, did not tell the family this news. She found it amusing that this happened. (Meade recalled that when she was met at the airport by Helen and her husband, Robert, they were surprised that she was not Black. They erroneously believed she was a representative from the NAACP.)[4]

When Meade's book was released in early 1988, the news got out that the ashes had never been properly interred. O'Dwyer, eighty years old at that time, was compelled to act. But instead of calling the Iveson family, he called the press.[5] Instead of asking Parker's family what they would like to do with the cremains, he asked gossip columnist Liz Smith. O'Dwyer carried the urn to the Algonquin Hotel for a wine and cheese media event on March 16, 1988. O'Dwyer didn't invite the Iveson family, but he did invite the Associated Press.

At the Algonquin, an informal gathering was held, drinks were served, and the urn was displayed. O'Dwyer turned over Parker's ashes to Dr. Benjamin Hooks, executive director of the NAACP. Dr. Hooks graciously accepted the ashes and promised to create a proper memorial for this inveterate New Yorker. The ashes were carried to Baltimore by a trusted member of the organization, Mildred Bond Roxborough, who happened to be the aunt of civil rights leader Julian Bond, later to be group's chairman in 1998.

On October 20, 1988, the ashes were placed in a shady spot outside the NAACP national headquarters in the Lochearn neighborhood of Baltimore, at **4805 Mount Hope Drive**. Dr. Hooks officiated over the dedication. The circular brick memorial designed by Harry G. Robinson was meant to recall the Round Table. The memorial stood in a small grove of pine trees. An urn containing Parker's ashes was lowered deep into the ground. A plaque was affixed, reading: "Here lie the ashes of Dorothy Parker (1893–1967). Humorist, writer, critic, defender of human and civil rights. For her epitaph she suggested 'Excuse My Dust.' This memorial garden is dedicated to her noble spirit which celebrated the oneness of humankind, and to the bonds of everlasting friendship between black and Jewish people." The ceremony was attended by O'Dwyer, city officials, and members of the NAACP staff. No New York reporters were in attendance, and the Iveson family wasn't contacted. They learned about it years later. Meade didn't make the trip. Dorothy Parker joined another former New Yorker, Edgar Allan Poe, in Baltimore guide books of famous gravesites. The 1980s turned into the 1990s, when interest in Dorothy Parker swelled.

From Baltimore Back to New York

Meanwhile, in early 2006, the NAACP hinted about moving the organization's national offices from Baltimore to Washington, DC, to be inside the Beltway. If the NAACP moved, what would happen to Dorothy Parker's ashes? Chairman Julian Bond told the *Baltimore Sun*: "Of course, we would no more think of abandoning these ashes than jumping off the top of the Empire State Building."[6] Bond sent a letter to the nine-year-old Dorothy Parker Society that the NAACP would contact the family if a move was planned. In February 2007 Barack Obama, then a junior United States senator from Illinois, announced his candidacy for president. Upon his election in 2008, the NAACP stayed in Baltimore.

Meanwhile, the family of Helen and Robert Iveson waited. The Dorothy Parker Society waited. Then, in June 2019 during the centennial of the first gathering of the Algonquin Round Table, the next step was taken—fifty-two years after Parker's death. Sisters

122 | Dorothy Parker's New York

Nancy Arcaro, Susan Cotton, and Joan Grossman are the grand-nieces of Dorothy Parker. Their great-grandparents are Henry and Eliza Rothschild. Their great-great-grandparents are Thomas and Ellen Marston. The trio travelled to Manhattan for the festivities at the New York Distilling Company and the Algonquin Hotel and decided to visit the family plot in Woodlawn Cemetery, in the Bronx, for the first time.

On a warm June afternoon, the sisters and friends from the Society took a train from Grand Central Terminal to the Woodlawn station, the same route Dorothy Rothschild and her siblings took to visit their mother's grave in 1898. The small group walked the length of the cemetery, passing the graves of Herman Melville and James Montgomery Flagg along the way.

Back in 2007, Woodlawn historian Susan Olsen had completed research in the cemetery archives about the Rothschild lot in the Myrtle section. Olsen discovered that Dorothy Parker was the legal owner of the lot and that she had full burial privileges. Olsen sat with the three sisters and explained the history of Woodlawn and how the process to inter cremains could be carried out. What resonated most, she said, was that

Figure 47. Robert Harris puts the urn containing Dorothy Parker's cremains into a transfer case held by the author in Baltimore. Harris oversaw the crew that dismantled the memorial garden outside the former headquarters of the NAACP. *Source:* Laurie Gwen Shapiro. Used with permission.

Baltimore to the Bronx | 123

cemeteries are "a forever place." The sisters decided then that the wait had been long enough and contacted the NAACP to begin talking about moving Dorothy to the Bronx.

For the transfer to occur, the Dorothy Parker Society acquired Parker's probated 1965 will from New York County, notarized legal documents from the family and Woodlawn Cemetery, and signed papers from the NAACP. The costs were determined and plans were made. But when all was just about ready, the COVID-19 pandemic stopped the world.

Leaving Baltimore

Following the lifting of the COVID-19 travel ban, it was safe to travel to Baltimore. Unbeknownst to the family, the NAACP had moved out of their headquarters to an office building elsewhere in Baltimore. The timing of the transfer was fortuitous. On August 18, 2020, a crew removed Parker's urn from underneath quite a bit of concrete. Shovels, picks, and an air hammer were required. A handful of staff from the NAACP were present. Baltimore attorney Ned T. Himmelrich looked on. He joked he worked "low bono" on Parker's intellectual property for twenty years for the NAACP. *The New Yorker* sent writer Laurie Gwen Shapiro. Everyone wore masks. The two hours of work got the urn into a plain, pine box.

Janette McCarthy Louard, NAACP deputy general counsel, led with remarks saying that Dorothy Parker was returning home. Rabbi Floyd L. Herman of Har Sinai Congregation, a Reform Jewish synagogue located in Owings Mills, Maryland, was the sole religious presence in the quiet garden. Rabbi Herman was also at the 1988 ceremony, when the ashes were put into the memorial. The rabbi said the Kaddish and wished Dorothy Parker a safe journey home.

Parker's ashes were next on the move to Baltimore Penn Station for the three-hour Amtrak ride home to Manhattan. In her first Uber ride, Dorothy's urn was driven through her old Upper West Side neighborhood.

Welcome to the Bronx

The next part of the journey was to bring Parker's urn to **Woodlawn Cemetery, 4199 Webster Avenue, Bronx, New York**. There was a summer rain shower on the anniversary of Parker's birthday on August 22, 2020. However, as soon as the brief remarks concluded, the sunshine burst out. Because of the ongoing pandemic, the sisters and their families could not travel to New York City. The Dorothy Parker Society represented the family for a simple graveside ceremony. The Society oversaw the small affair, which had less than twelve people in attendance.

Figure 48. Woodlawn Cemetery boasts more than 1,300 mausoleums and attracts more than 100,000 visitors annually. The landscaping and architecture are by iconic names. *Source:* Photo by the author.

A Visit to Woodlawn Cemetery

A visit to Dorothy Parker's final resting place in Woodlawn Cemetery, the Bronx, is a must for any fans in New York. It is easy to get there via mass transit or car and is open seven days a week from 8:30 a.m. to 4:30 p.m.

In 1863 the Board of Trustees purchased more than three hundred acres of farmland dating to the Colonial era. The first burial was in 1865, three months before the Civil War ended. Only a quarter of the land was forest; the rest had been farmed for generations. It was laid out by notable landscape architect James Charles Sidney. The New York and Harlem Railroad operated trains directly from Manhattan to Woodlawn. A special funeral car ran from Grand Central Terminal; in 1903 it could be rented for $50 ($1,400 today) to transport mourners roundtrip. Horse-drawn carriages took mourning parties directly from the train station to the gravesites. By 1909, only forty-four years later, there were 66,000 burials. The grounds were expanded to four hundred acres.

The Gilded Age brought many prominent families to Woodlawn, as well as scores of Civil War veterans (both the blue and the gray). Admiral David Glasgow Farragut was a household name when he was buried in Woodlawn in 1870, with President Ulysses S. Grant making the train trip to the burial. The twentieth century saw hundreds of show business names come to Woodlawn, as well as six mayors and three senators. Today there are more than 310,000 souls buried in the park-like setting, which is half the size of Central Park.

Woodlawn was designated a National Historic Landmark in 2011, partly due to its approximately 1,300 private mausoleums, the most significant collection in the United States. Designed by architects like John Russell Pope (the Jefferson Memorial), McKim, Mead and White (Prospect Park), and Cass Gilbert (the Woolworth Building), they contain stained glass from Tiffany. and rival John LaFarge. The mausoleums are surrounded by gardens designed by the Olmsted Brothers and Beatrix Farrand.

The only other member of the Algonquin Round Table buried in Woodlawn is writer Peggy Leech, who is next to her husband, publisher Ralph Pulitzer, and father-in-law, Joseph Pulitzer. Among the notable mausoleums are the grand one for Oliver Hazard Perry Belmont and Alva Erskine Stirling Smith Belmont.

Among the famous names in the landmark cemetery are Irving Berlin, Nellie Bly (pseudonym of Elizabeth Cochrane), Carrie Chapman Catt, George M. Cohan, Countee Cullen, Miles Davis, Duke Ellington, Fiorello La Guardia, John Held Jr., Herman Melville, Grantland Rice, and Madame C. J. Walker. Many of the stars that Parker reviewed in Broadway playhouses are also in Woodlawn, such as Nora Bayes and Bert Williams. But the name that draws many kindred spirits is "Professor" Jerry Thomas (in the Poplar section). The June 1862 *Harper's Weekly* carried an ad for his book *How to Mix Drinks: Containing Recipes for Mixing American, English, French, German, Italian, Spanish, and Russian Drinks*. This was the first bartenders' guide.

Getting There: Know that there are two gates into Woodlawn: the Webster Avenue Gate and the Jerome Avenue entrance. Parker's grave is a short walk from the Webster entrance; it is approximately a one-mile walk from the Jerome Avenue entry.

By Train: Metro North runs to Woodlawn Station. Take the Harlem Line local train (North White Plains). The cemetery is across Webster Avenue. It is about a twenty-five-minute trip from Grand Central Terminal.

By Subway: Take the number 2 or number 5 train to 233rd Street Station. Walk three blocks along 233rd, downhill. Cross over Webster Avenue. It is a half-mile walk to the Webster gate, which is closest to Dorothy Parker. The number 4 Train to Woodlawn Station will put you across the street from Woodlawn Cemetery's gate on Jerome Avenue; then, walk approximately one mile along Central Avenue to the Myrtle Section. Free maps are available at the cemetery offices.

By Car: Set GPS to 4199 Webster Avenue, Bronx, New York 10470. The cemetery is off the Bronx River Parkway.

Visit woodlawn.org to plan your visit, and tell the staff you are there to visit Dorothy Parker. Bring roses.

The NAACP was represented by Dr. Hazel Nell Dukes, president of the NAACP New York State Conference and a member of the NAACP National Board of Directors, and a member of the NAACP Executive Committee. "I was thinking last night. As we look at New York and the world, the Association was founded here, on Fifth Avenue, so it is no coincidence that she wanted to come home to New York," Dukes said. "It's our home too, founded here in 1909. So, we are here bringing this great, honorable woman who gave to the cause when it was not popular. It was not popular at the time that Dorothy Parker began to associate with the NAACP. There were many names called, as we see today, [such as] communists. People who wanted to assist those who were less fortunate. I'm honored to be here today to welcome her home, back to New York, the founding of the NAACP. The late Dr. Benjamin Hooks always said, 'Whatever you do, don't bother Dorothy Parker.' He made that very clear. We welcome you home, and we thank you for all you've done, and your spirit will continue to lead us in the country to be better than what we have been and what we know we can be."[7]

Among the speakers was historian Susan Olsen welcoming Dorothy Parker to her final resting place. "Today is one of the most neat days, as we bring somebody back," Olsen said. "Many of Parker's contemporaries, those who she had accolades for, and barbs for, and cocktails with, are here at Woodlawn. She has finally come home not only to be with her family but also to be with the people that she loved, criticized, supported, and she saluted in her days at the Algonquin."

The hole was dug closest to Eliza Rothschild, who young Dorothy Rothschild had lost when she was just four years old. A team member from Woodlawn placed the box into the ground; the box had a small gold plaque on top:

Dorothy R. Parker

1893–1967

"Excuse My Dust"

The attendees were invited to shovel scoops of New York City dirt onto the simple pine box. Society member William Zeffiro sang acapella "I Wished on the Moon," the 1929 song that Parker wrote for the Cecil B. DeMille film *Dynamite*. Next, rather than read a Parker poem at her own ceremony, the Society chose a poem by another New York poet who is a permanent resident of Woodlawn, Countee Cullen, to welcome her home. His 1915 poem "I Have a Rendezvous with Life" was read:

I Have a Rendezvous with Life

I have a rendezvous with Life
In days I hope will come

Ere youth has sped and strength of mind,
Ere voices sweet grown dumb;
I have a rendezvous with Life
When Spring's first heralds hum.
It may be I shall greet her soon,
Shall riot at her behest;
It may be I shall seek in vain
The peace of her downy breast;
Yet I would keep this rendezvous,
And deem all hardships sweet,
If at the end of the long white way,
There Life and I shall meet.
Sure some will cry it better far
To crown their days in sleep,
Than face the wind, the road, and rain,
To heed the falling deep;
Though wet, nor blow, nor space I fear,
Yet fear I deeply, too,
Lest Death shall greet and claim me ere
I keep Life's rendezvous.

The Gravestone, the Inscription

The news of Parker's return to her hometown spread internationally. The descendants of Dorothy's beloved niece, Helen Droste Iveson, were prepared to commission a gravestone. However, fans clamored to be a part of this process, and some asked where they could donate money. So, the Dorothy Parker Memorial Fund was created to raise funds for a bit grander gravestone. The New York Distilling Company made a small batch of Dorothy Parker Gin; the Al Hirschfeld Foundation granted permission for artwork to be used. The gin sold out in two days, and the funds were used for the gravestone.

These are the five choices of the design: The circular flowers surrounding Parker's name are evening primrose. This is a nod to one of her most famous poems:

The Evening Primrose
You know the bloom, unearthly white,
That none has seen by morning light –
The tender moon, alone, may bare
Its beauty to the secret air.
Who'd venture past its dark retreat
Must kneel, for holy things and sweet,

Figure 49. The gravestone dedicated to Parker in 2021 attracts visitors from around the globe who bring roses, just like Dorothy Parker asks in "Epitaph for a Darling Lady." *Source:* Photo by the author.

That blossom, mystically blown,
No man may gather for his own
Nor touch it, lest it droop and fall. . . .
Oh, I am not like that at all!

The shape of the gravestone is an homage to another gravestone in Woodlawn (in the Oakwood Plot): Mayor Fiorello La Guardia, who Parker campaigned for. The half-round top adds a whimsical touch. The letters are in an art deco style, popular in the 1920s and 1930s, also Parker's heyday.

The inscription was chosen by the family from among several poems. The famous "Excuse My Dust" line was not chosen; that is inscribed on a small gold plaque attached to the box containing the urn. Care went into the choice of the inscription, and it came down to "Epitaph for a Darling Lady," which Parker gave to her mentor, Franklin P. Adams. He published it in the *World* on August 3, 1925, when Parker was thirty-one years old. Carved in stone are the last four lines:

All her hours were yellow sands,
Blown in foolish whorls and tassels;

Baltimore to the Bronx | 129

Slipping warmly through her hands;
Patted into little castles.

Shiny day on shiny day
Tumble in a rainbow clutter,
As she flipped them all away,
Sent them spinning down the gutter.

Leave for her a red young rose,
Go your way, and save your pity;
She is happy, for she knows
That her dust is very pretty.

Finally, the family chose the placement of the grave. Dorothy Parker's urn was placed next to her mother, Eliza. The gravestone was unveiled by Parker's family and the Society in time for her birthday on August 22, 2021.

The gravesite is easy to locate, near the gates on Webster Avenue, in the Myrtle section.

Dorothy Parker, from Tattoos to Instagram

With Dorothy Parker back in hometown, we have a chance to reflect on her legacy. Since her death in the summer of 1967, Parker has become a figure of romance, beloved by the cocktail crowd and hailed for her witty repartee.

Since 1967, Dorothy Parker has achieved icon status. Not a month goes by that a one-woman show of her work isn't performed on a stage, be it in Seattle or Sydney. Parker's lifestyle was featured in Aviva Slesin's 1987 film *The Ten Year Lunch: The Wit and Legend of the Algonquin Round Table*, which earned an Academy Award for best documentary. But probably the biggest pop-culture boost to the Parker myth came from the 1994 independent feature film *Mrs. Parker and the Vicious Circle*, directed by Alan Rudolph and starring Jennifer Jason Leigh as Parker and Campbell Scott as Robert Benchley. Leigh won best actress from the National Society of Film Critics and was nominated for a Golden Globe. The screenplay, which appears to have been lifted almost entirely from Marion Meade's biography, portrays Dorothy as a lovable sad sack. The film enjoyed moderate success, and its thirty years on television have exposed Parker to a new audience.

Since Parker's death, New York has undergone another of its continual rebirths. Her old neighborhood, the Upper West Side, was on the skids in the 1960s and 1970s but came back and was gentrified; it is now one of the top ten richest neighborhoods in Manhattan.[8] The playhouses she frequented on Broadway are still there, although numerous theaters were razed by developers in the 1980s. As this guide shows, the majority of her apartments are still standing, as are many of the spots that she frequented.

The Algonquin Hotel has transformed itself into a veritable hall of fame for Parker and her friends, naming drinks and entrées after them and hosting book parties, magazine launches, and publishing seminars. The owners hung a beautiful oil painting of the Round Table by Natalie Ascencios in the hotel. Prints by Al Hirschfeld line the walls. A suite is named for her.

Parker's books remain in print and selling well, a sign of the worth of any notable writer. All of her poetry and short fiction is available in bookstores today. A newspaper writer seeking the easy pun or turn of phrase invokes her name practically every day. Fans have gotten so many tattoos inspired by Dorothy, there is a gallery on dorothyparker.com. She leads Instagram in quotes and memes. Of all the Round Table members, she has become the most successful in death. The city that she wrote about—gin-soaked and moody, bustling and raucous—lives on today in the hearts and imaginations of readers as well as those who walk in Dorothy Parker's hometown.

The Legacy

In 1993 the U.S. Postal Service honored Parker with a commemorative postage stamp on the centennial of her birth. Her birthplace, **732 Ocean Avenue, Long Branch, New Jersey**, was named a national literary landmark in 2005. In 2009 the Museum of the City of New York, to mark the 400th anniversary of explorer Henry Hudson's arrival, named Parker to the list of "The New York City 400" movers and shakers. She is a member of the New Jersey Hall of Fame and the New York State Writers Hall of Fame. Dorothy Parker Gin was launched in Brooklyn in 2011, and it is wildly successful; wags say the distillery does more to promote Parker than her publishers.

The Dorothy Parker Society launched in 1999 and counts fans around the world, offers walking tours covering sites important to Dorothy Parker and her pals, and gathers to toast her birthday. Parker herself might have commented on this activity with a typical sardonic observation, but no doubt she would also be pleased with the upsurge of enthusiasm for her work, which has introduced many adoring fans to the Manhattan she called home. In 1928 she crafted an essay called "My Home Town," which is just as epic as E. B. White's "Here Is New York." Parker concludes:

London is satisfied, Paris is resigned, but New York is always hopeful. Always it believes that something particularly good is about to come off, and it must hurry to meet it. There is excitement ever running in its streets. Each day, as you go out, you feel the little nervous quiver that is yours when you sit in a theater just before the curtain rises. Other places may give you a sweet and soothing sense of level; but in New York, there is always the feeling of "Something's going to happen." It isn't peace. But, you know, you do get used to peace, and so quickly. And you never get used to New York.

Figure 50. Dorothy Parker and Alan Campbell are welcomed back to Hollywood, September 1936. They were working for studio boss David O. Selznick at the time. *Source:* Dorothy Parker Society Archive.

Dorothy Parker Timeline

1893   August 22, Dorothy Rothschild is born to Eliza "Annie" Marston and Jacob Henry Rothschild at their summer beach house in West End, New Jersey.

1898   July 20, Dorothy's mother dies in West End.

1900   Henry Rothschild marries Eleanor Frances Lewis in January.

1900   Dorothy begins attending Catholic elementary school at Blessed Sacrament Academy on West 79th Street.

1903   Stepmother Eleanor dies in April.

1907   Dorothy enrolls at Miss Dana's, a girls' finishing school, Morristown, New Jersey. She leaves after less than a year, ending her formal education at age fourteen.

1913   December 27, Henry Rothschild dies.

1914   Dorothy goes to California with her friend, socialite Frances H. Billings. The following year, Dorothy is her maid of honor; in the wedding party is future husband Edwin "Eddie" Pond Parker II.

1915   *Vanity Fair* publishes Dorothy's first piece of light verse, "Any Porch," in the September issue. She earns twelve dollars and starts her literary career. Later is hired by *Vogue* as a junior staff member.

1917   July 2, Dorothy marries Eddie Parker, a stockbroker from Hartford, Connecticut, in a civil ceremony in Yonkers, Westchester County, New York. She is twenty-three; he is twenty-six.

1917	Eddie leaves for army ambulance training in New Jersey and is later sent to France with the American Expeditionary Forces (AEF). He serves in combat until the end of the war. Returns February 1919.
1918	Dorothy becomes New York's first female drama critic, writing for *Vanity Fair*.
1919	The Algonquin Round Table is formed in June at a luncheon to welcome back *New York Times* drama critic Alexander Woollcott from AEF service.
1920	Fired from *Vanity Fair* in January. That same month Prohibition begins in the United States.
1920	Robert Benchley and Dorothy rent an office together in the Metropolitan Opera House building and embark on freelance writing careers.
1921	Dorothy sells her first short fiction piece, "Sorry, the Line Is Busy," to *Life* in April.
1922	Dorothy and Eddie separate. Dorothy dates Chicago newspaperman Charles MacArthur.
1922	Has an abortion.
1923	First suicide attempt.
1924	With playwright Elmer Rice, Dorothy writes her first play, *Close Harmony*; it flops.
1924	Eddie moves home to Connecticut; Dorothy does not join him.
1925	*The New Yorker* debuts in February; Dorothy writes the first drama review for cofounders Harold Ross and Jane Grant. She begins a thirty-year relationship with the magazine.
1925	August 16, Franklin P. Adams is given—for free—six poems in Parker's "Some Beautiful Letters" series. The *New York World* publishes "Observation," "Social Note," "News Item," "Interview," "Comment," and "Résumé."
1926	Attempts suicide by overdosing on the sedative Veronal.
1926	First trip to Europe, traveling with Ernest Hemingway and Robert Benchley.
1926	Her first collection of verse is released. *Enough Rope* is a smash hit.
1927	Dorothy travels to Boston to protest the pending execution of anarchists Nicola Sacco and Bartolomeo Vanzetti.
1928	*Sunset Gun* is published, her second collection of verse.

1928	Divorce from Eddie Parker is finalized; she keeps his name.
1929	*Bookman* publishes "Big Blonde," her novella based on her suicide attempt. The story wins the O. Henry Award.
1929	Dorothy takes a second European trip, spending most of her time with Sara and Gerald Murphy's family in Switzerland.
1930	Dorothy's short fiction is collected and published as *Laments for the Living*.
1931	Her third and final collection of light verse is published. *Death and Taxes* sells fewer copies than the previous two books.
1932	Dorothy makes one more attempt at suicide.
1933	Meets Alan Campbell, an actor and writer from Virginia who is eleven years her junior.
1933	Her collected short stories are published as *After Such Pleasures*.
1934	June 18, Dorothy and Alan marry in Raton, New Mexico. They live in Denver, Colorado, while Alan acts in summer theater. The couple moves to Hollywood in September to write for Paramount.
1936	Dorothy and Alan buy a 111-acre farm in Bucks County, Pennsylvania. They renovate a colonial farmhouse, their part-time home for the next nine years. Asked to describe her farm in two words, Dorothy replies, "Want it?"
1937	Dorothy and Alan are nominated for an Academy Award for writing the film *A Star Is Born*.
1937	The couple sail to Spain and witness the civil war firsthand while in Madrid and Valencia. On returning to New York in October, Parker begins fundraising for Spanish hospitals. The following year, Dorothy writes "Soldiers of the Republic" about her experience in Spain.
1942	Alan enlists in the U.S. Army Air Forces. He accepts an officer's commission and is sent to London. The couple are apart for nearly five years.
1944	Dorothy publishes her last piece of poetry, the strange "War Song," which appears in *The New Yorker*.
1944	Viking publishes *The Portable Dorothy Parker*, a collection of her verse and short fiction. It has never gone out of print.
1946	Alan returns from duty overseas; the couple splits.

1947   Dorothy is nominated for an Academy Award for cowriting *Smash-Up: The Story of a Woman*, a vehicle for Susan Hayward.

1949–50 Dorothy hooks up with Ross Evans, twenty-four years her junior. They cowrite *The Coast of Illyria*, which is produced in Dallas but doesn't make it to Broadway. They also write "The Game" for *Cosmopolitan*. Evans and Parker split up in Mexico.

1950   Dorothy and Alan reunite and remarry in Los Angeles.

1951   United Artists produces *Queen for a Day*, a movie based on her 1932 short story "Horsie."

1951   Dorothy and Alan separate again; she moves back to New York.

1952–53 She collaborates with Arnaud d'Usseau on *The Ladies of the Corridor*, produced at the Longacre Theatre for just forty-five performances.

1955   Dorothy is called before a New York state legislative committee and asked about her politics. Parker invokes the Fifth Amendment when asked directly if she is a Communist.

1958   *Esquire* publishes Dorothy's last short story, "The Bolt Behind the Blue," in December; she begins reviewing books for the magazine.

1958   The National Institute of Arts and Letters gives Dorothy the Marjorie Peabody Waite Award for her contribution to American literature.

1961   Returns to Alan and Los Angeles. They reside at 8983 Norma Place, West Hollywood.

1961   Dorothy does her last movie work on the unproduced feature *The Good Soup* for Twentieth-Century Fox.

1963   Alan dies of an overdose at home in West Hollywood; the coroner's report lists the death as a probable suicide.

1964   Dorothy returns to New York City and resides on the Upper East Side.

1967   June 7, Parker dies at her apartment in the Volney Hotel. She is seventy-three years old. Her death makes international news and Walter Cronkite reports it on the *CBS Evening News*.

1988   Parker's ashes, held at the offices of her attorney, Paul O'Dwyer, are turned over to the NAACP. On October 20 they are placed in a memorial garden outside the organization's headquarters in Baltimore, Maryland.

1992	The U.S. Postal Service issues a commemorative stamp in West End, New Jersey, Parker's birthplace.
1998	The Dorothy Parker Society is formed.
2005	Her birthplace at 732 Ocean Avenue, Long Branch, New Jersey, is declared a national literary landmark. In 2014 Parker is inducted into the New Jersey Hall of Fame.
2011	She is inducted into the New York State Writers Hall of Fame.
2011	Dorothy Parker American Gin debuts from the New York Distilling Co. in Brooklyn.
2020	On her birthday, Parker's cremains are interred next to her parents and grandparents in Woodlawn Cemetery, the Bronx. Her gravestone is dedicated exactly one year later in the Myrtle section.

Notes

Chapter 1

1. Dorothy Parker, "My Hometown," *McCall's*, 1928.
2. Dorothy Parker, "Mr. Durant," *American Mercury*, September 1924, 81.
3. Robert E. Drennan, *The Algonquin Wits* (Secaucus, NJ: Citadel Press, 1968), 123.
4. Marion Meade, *Dorothy Parker: What Fresh Hell Is This?* (New York: Villard, 1988), 32.
5. Dorothy Rothschild, *Vanity Fair*, September 1915, 32.
6. Dorothy Parker, "Coda," *New York World*, March 22, 1928, 13.
7. Dorothy Parker, "Women: A Hate Song," Vanity Fair, August 1916, 61.

Chapter 2

1. Dorothy Parker, "Dorothy Parker," in *Writers at Work: The Paris Review Interviews*, ed. Malcolm Cowley (New York: Viking Press, 1958), 76.
2. Marion Meade, *Dorothy Parker: What Fresh Hell Is This?* (New York: Villard, 1988), 8.
3. Wyatt Cooper, "Whatever You Think Dorothy Parker Was Like, She Wasn't," *Esquire*, July 1968, 57.
4. Dorothy Rothschild, letter to Henry Rothschild, June 1906, collection of Joan Grossman, Nancy Arcaro, Susan Cotton.
5. Dorothy Parker, "Apartment House Anthology," *Saturday Evening Post*, August 20, 1921, 10.
6. John Keats, *You Might As Well Live: The Life and Times of Dorothy Parker* (New York: Simon and Schuster, 1970), 32.

Chapter 3

1. Author interview with Stuart Y. Silverstein.
2. Dorothy Parker, "Soldiers of the Republic," *New Yorker*, February 5, 1933, 13.

3. Marion Meade, *Bobbed Hair and Bathtub Gin: Writers Running Wild in the Twenties* (New York: Nan A. Talese/Doubleday, 2004), 3.

4. Dorothy Parker, "The Conning Tower," *New York World*, July 31, 1925, 11.

5. Marilyn Kaytor, *"21": The Life and Times of New York's Favorite Club* (New York: Viking Adult, 1975), 13.

6. Gordon Kahn and Al Hirschfeld, *The Speakeasies of 1932* (New York: Applause Theatre and Cinema Books, 2004.

7. Dorothy Parker, "The Small Hours," *Vanity Fair*, April 26, 1926, 64.

8. Helen Droste, telegram to Seward Collins, March 25, 1927, Seward Collins Papers. Yale Collection of American Literature, Beinecke Rare Book and Manuscript Library.

9. Courtesy of Nancy Arcaro, Susan Cotton, and Joan Grossman.

Chapter 4

1. All theater reviews in chapter 4 appear in *Dorothy Parker, Complete Broadway, 1918–1923* (New York: iUniverse, 2010) and *The Portable Dorothy Parker* (New York: Penguin Books, 2006).

2. Dorothy Parker, *Not Much Fun: The Lost Poems of Dorothy Parker*, ed. Stuart Y. Silverstein (New York: Scribner, 1996), 115.

3. Dorothy Parker, "Dorothy Parker," in *Writers at Work: The Paris Review Interviews*, ed. Malcolm Cowley (New York: Viking Press, 1958), 76.

Chapter 5

1. Randall Calhoun, *Dorothy Parker: A Bio-Bibliography* (Westport, CT: Greenwood Press, 1993), 20.

2. Robert E. Drennan, *The Algonquin Wits* (Secaucus, NJ: Citadel Press, 1968), 116.

3. "'Guests' Aiding Strike Beaten at the Waldorf," *New York Times*, February 7, 1934, 1.

4. "Overflow Rally Spurs Nelson Fight," *Daily Worker*, July 28, 1952.

5. "Dottie Parker Didn't Ask Where $$ Went," *New York News*, February 26, 1955.

Chapter 6

1. Marion Meade, *Dorothy Parker: What Fresh Hell Is This?* (New York: Villard, 1988), 392.

2. Alden Whitman, "Dorothy Parker, 73, Literary Wit, Dies," *New York Times*, June 8, 1967, 1.

3. Meade, *Dorothy Parker*, 412.

Chapter 7

1. Dorothy Parker, will dated February 6, 1965, File No. 3819/1967, Surrogate's Court, County of New York, New York, Hon. S. Samuel DiFalco, Surrogate.

2. Dorothy Parker, will dated February 6, 1965.

3. Author interview with Susan Cotton, August 2019.

4. Author interview with Marion Meade.

5. Liz Smith, letter to author.

6. Rob Hiaasen, "Fans Hope Writer's Ashes Won't Be Left in the Dust," *Baltimore Sun*, May 28, 2006, 1A.

7. Transcript by Laurie Gwen Shapiro, provided to author.

8. Amy Plitt, "The Richest Neighborhoods in New York City," NY Curbed, December 27, 2019.

For Further Reading

Adler, Polly. *A House Is Not a Home*. New York: Rinehart, 1953.

Applegate, Debby. *Madam: The Biography of Polly Adler, Icon of the Jazz Age*. New York: Knopf, 2022.

Ashley, Sally. *F.P.A.: The Life and Times of Franklin Pierce Adams*. New York: Beaufort Books, 1986.

Benchley, Nat, and Kevin C. Fitzpatrick. *The Lost Algonquin Round Table: Humor, Fiction, Journalism, Criticism and Poetry From America's Most Famous Literary Circle*. New York: iUniverse, 2009.

Benchley, Nathaniel. *Robert Benchley: A Biography*. New York: McGraw-Hill, 1955.

Botto, Louis. *At This Theatre: 100 Years of Broadway Shows, Stories and Stars*. New York: Applause Theatre and Cinema Books, 2002.

Burrows, Edwin G., and Mike Wallace. *Gotham: A History of New York City to 1898*. New York: Oxford University Press, 1999.

Calhoun, Randall. *Dorothy Parker: A Bio-Bibliography*. Westport, CT: Greenwood Press, 1993.

Connelly, Marc. *Voices Offstage*. New York: Holt, Rinehart and Winston, 1968.

Case, Frank. *Tales of a Wayward Inn*. New York: Frederick A. Stokes Company, 1938.

Dolkart, Andrew. *Guide to New York City Landmarks*. New York: John Wiley and Sons, 1998.

Drennan, Robert E. *The Algonquin Wits*. Reprint, Secaucus, NJ: Citadel Press, 1985.

Ellis, Edward Robb. *The Epic of New York City*. New York: Marboro, 1966.

Fitzpatrick, Kevin C. *The Algonquin Round Table New York, A Historical Guide*. Guilford, CT: Lyons Press, 2015.

———. *Under the Table: A Dorothy Parker Cocktail Guide*. Guilford, CT: Lyons Press, 2013.

Frewin, Leslie. *The Late Mrs. Dorothy Parker*. New York: Macmillan, 1987.

Gaines, James R. *Wit's End: Days and Nights of the Algonquin Round Table*. New York: Harcourt, 1977.

Grant, Jane. *Ross, The New Yorker, and Me*. New York: Reynal, 1968.

Harriman, Margaret Case. *The Vicious Circle*. New York: Rinehart, 1951.

Kahn, Gordon, and Al Hirschfeld. *The Speakeasies of 1932*. New York: Applause Theatre and Cinema Books, 2004.

Keats, John. *You Might As Well Live: The Life and Times of Dorothy Parker*. New York: Simon and Schuster, 1970.

Meade, Marion. *Dorothy Parker: What Fresh Hell Is This?* New York: Villard, 1988.

New Jersey Writers Project. *Entertaining a Nation: The Career of Long Branch.* Long Branch, NJ: Works Projects Administration, 1939.

Parker, Dorothy. *Complete Broadway, 1918–1923.* New York: iUniverse, 2010.

———. *Complete Poems.* New York: Penguin Books, 1999.

———. *Complete Stories.* New York: Penguin Books, 2005.

———. *Not Much Fun: The Lost Poems of Dorothy Parker.* Edited by Stuart Y. Silverstein. New York: Scribner, 1996.

———. *The Portable Dorothy Parker.* New York: Penguin Books, 1944.

Thurber, James. *Men, Women, and Dogs.* New York: Harcourt, Brace, 1943.

———. *The Years with Ross.* New York: Little, Brown, 1959.

Trager, James. *The New York Chronology.* New York: HarperCollins, 2003.

Index

Abraham Lincoln (Drinkwater), 84
Abraham Lincoln Brigade, 92, 103
Actors' Equity Association, 89
Adams, Franklin P. (FPA), 17, 37, 38, 43, 45, 58, 120, 129, 134, 143
Adams, Maude, 22, 27, 28, 71
Adams, Robert, 81
Adding Machine, The (Rice), 83
Adler, Polly, 49, 143
Adler, Richard, 112
Admirable Crichton, The (Barrie), 75
After Such Pleasures (1933, 1940), 3, 13, 81, 135
Ainslee's, 69, 70, 79
Algonquin Hotel (59 West 44th Street), xi, 10, 17, 36, 37, 42–47, 57, 66, 100, 121–123, 130
Algonquin Round Table, 10, 37, 40–47, 58, 66, 79, 88, 122, 129
  Demise, 93
  Dorothy Parker membership of, 10, 37
  Founding, 43, 134
Al Hirschfeld Foundation, The, ix, 128
Al Hirschfeld Theatre (302-14 West 45th Street), 82–83
Allen, Vera, 87
American Council on Soviet Relations, 92, 102
American Mercury, 6, 13

Amtrak, xi, 124
"An Apartment House Anthology" (1921), 29
An Ideal Husband (Wilde), 74
Anderson, Marian, 101
Anderson, Sherwood, 43
Animal Crackers (Kaufman and Ryskind), 72, 79
animals, D. P. fondness for, 17, 32, 105
Anna Christie (O'Neill), 85
Ansonia Apartment Hotel (2108 Broadway), 20, 51
"Any Porch" (1915), 9, 22, 34, 133
Apollo Theatre/Lyric Theatre (223 West 42nd Street), 71, 77
Arbuckle, Roscoe "Fatty," 116
Arcaro, Nancy, 1x, 123
Arno, Peter, 77, 115
"Arrangement in Black and White" (1927) 10, 53, 105
Ascencios, Natalie, 131
Astaire, Adele, 71
Astaire, Fred, 71
Astor Hotel/Astor Bar. *See* Hotel Astor
Astor, John Jacob IV, 60, 66
Atkinson, Brooks, 87
Auchincloss, Louis, 112

Baldwin, James, 2, 120
"Ballade at Thirty-Five" (1924), 42

Baltimore, xi, 2, 122–124, 136
Baltimore Sun, 122
"Banquet of Crow, The" (1957), 54
Bar Association (42 West 44th Street), 46
Baragwanath, Jack, 60
Barretts of Wimpole Street, The, 73
Barrie, James M., 27, 73, 75
Barry, Philip, 97
Barrymore, Ethel, 43, 45, 62, 71, 89
Barrymore, Lionel, 89
Basquiat, Jean-Michel, 117
Beatles, the, 55
Beck, Martin, 82, 83
Behan, Brendan, 43
Belasco, David, 78–79, 86
Belasco Theatre (111 West 44th Street), 17,
    71, 78, 79
Belmont, Alva Erskine Stirling Smith, 126
Belmont, August, 20
Belmont, Oliver Hazard Perry, 126
Benchley, Gertrude, 41
Benchley, Robert, 17, 36, 40–41, 45, 58, 62,
    70, 73, 86, 91, 97, 98
  Early death, 60
  Friendship with D. P., 36, 40, 55, 59–60,
    83, 88, 94, 134
Berlin, Irving, 77, 86, 126
Berns, Charlie, 58
Bernstein, Leonard, 79
Bernstien, Oscar, 1, 120
  See O'Dwyer & Bernstien
Best, Edna, 87
"Big Blonde" (1928), 11, 41, 65, 93, 135
Bijou Theatre (209 West 45th Street), 81–82
Billings, Frances, 6, 133
Biltmore Hotel, 101
Blessed Sacrament Academy (168–70 West
    79th Street), 26, 133
Bly, Nellie, 4, 126
Bonanno, Joseph, 51
Bond, Julian, 122
Boni & Liveright (61 West 48th Street), 12,
    56–57
Bookman, The, 13, 41, 65, 135

Booth, Shirley, 81
Boston, 2, 87, 89, 91, 101, 134
Broadway. *See* theater district
"Broadway Massacre," 71
Bronx, The, 2, 123–130, 137
Brooks, Mel, 116
Broun, Heywood, 17, 30, 43–46, 53, 58, 77,
    91
Buchanan, Thompson, 80
Bucks County (Pennsylvania), 94, 135
Burke, Billie, 54, 75, 76
Burroughs, William S., 43

Caesar's Wife (Maugham), 54, 75
California, 5, 6, 16, 32, 65, 115, 133
  as California resident, 94, 113
Campbell, Alan (D. P. second husband), 10,
    54, 67, 94, 113, 132, 135
Campbell, Frank E., 117
  See Frank E. Campbell funeral home
Candide (Hellman), 83
Capote, Truman, 53, 54, 111
Carroll, Harry, 85
Caruso, Enrico, 60
Case, Frank, 46, 46
"Cassandra Drops into Verse" (1925), 53
Catt, Carrie Chapman, 126
Cavett, Frank, 94
Central Park, 1, 20, 26–32, 54, 56, 59, 111,
    114, 126
Cerf, Bennett, 57, 112
Chambers, Whittaker, 101, 102
Chanin, Irwin S., 29
Chapman, John, 87
Charles Hopkins Theatre (155 West 49th
    Street), 89
Chase, Edna Woolman, 35
Chasen's, 60
Cheever, John, 53
Chelsea Hotel, 43
child labor, 4–5
Civil War Monument (Riverside Park), 31–32
Close Harmony (Parker and Rice), 83, 134
"Club Row" (44th Street), 37, 46

"Coda" (1928), 11

Cohan, George M., 60, 77, 126

Collected Poems: Not So Deep a Well (1936), 13

Collins, Seward, 41, 65

Comedy Theatre (110 West 41st Street), 74

"Comment" (1925), 39, 134

Commodore Hotel, 99–100

Communist Party, 91, 102, 104–106, 121, 126–127, 136

Condé Nast Publications, 6, 13, 22, 35, 36, 54

Coney Island, 47–48

Connelly, Marc, 52, 60, 88, 94

Cooper, Anderson Hays, 117

Cooper, Wyatt, 26, 111, 112, 117

Cornell Club (6 East 44th Street), 46

Cort, John, 84

Cort Theatre (138 West 48th Street), 17, 84

Cotton, Susan, 123

Counterattack, 104

COVID-19 pandemic, 1, 47, 89, 116, 124

Cowley, Malcolm, 102, 111

Crane, Hart, 57

Crane, Stephen, 4, 70

Crawford, Joan, 117

Crisis magazine, 105

Crowninshield, Frank, 34, 36, 37, 54, 69

Cullen, Countee, 126–128

cummings, e. e., 57

Dakota Apartments, 20, 29

Davis, Miles, 126

Dean, James, 26

Dear Brutus (Barrie), 73

Death and Taxes (1931), 11, 13, 66, 93, 135

Delamarre, Jacques, 29

De Los Rios, Fernando, 95

DeRosa, Eugene, 84

"Dialogue at Three in the Morning" (1926), 10, 53

Diary of Anne Frank, The, 84

Dix, Dorothy (Elizabeth Meriwether Gilmer), 70

dogs, D. P. love for, 17, 26, 29–33, 58, 67, 105, 115

Dorothy Parker: What Fresh Hell Is This? (Meade), 121

Dorothy Parker Gin, xi, 128, 131

Dorothy Parker Society, 30, 122, 124, 131, 137

Return of D. P. ashes, 124

Doubletree Metropolitan Hotel, 89

Dreiser, Theodore, 57, 70

Drew, John, 45

Drinkwater, John, 84

Droste, George Henry, 120

DuBois, W. E. B., 105

"Dusk Before Fireworks" (1932), 66

d'Usseau, Arnaud, 86, 87, 136

Dukes, Dr. Hazel, 127

Dynamite (1929), 127

Eiges, Sidney, 105

Eighteenth Amendment, 49, 51

Elitch Gardens (Denver), 67

Ellington, Duke, 126

Eloise (Plaza Hotel), 43, 55

Empire Theatre (1430 Broadway), 27, 73

Enough Rope (1926), 9, 11, 13, 57, 134

"Epitaph" (1925), 53

"Epitaph for a Darling Lady" (1925), 129

Equitable Building, 6

Esquire magazine, 106, 108–109, 112, 117, 136

Evans, Ross, 136

"Evening Primrose, The" (1929), 128

"Everlastin' Ingénue Blues" (1922), 86

Fairbanks, Douglas, 47

Farnham, Sally James, 65

Farrand, Beatrix, 126

Fast, Howard, 98, 104

Faulkner, William, 47, 57

Federal Bureau of Investigation (FBI)

alleged Communist sympathies, 102–106

D. P. membership dossier, 92–93, 102

Ferber, Edna, 17, 29, 45, 46, 52, 58, 94

Ferncliff Cemetery (Hartsdale), 117, 119, 120
Fields, Dorothy, 77
Fields, W. C., 70–72, 89
Fitzgerald, F. Scott, 9, 55, 58, 62, 67, 76, 101
Fitzgerald, Zelda, 9, 58, 62, 101
Flagg, James Montgomery, 123
Fleischmann, Raoul, 51, 53
44th Street Theatre (216 West 44th Street), 79
49th Street Theatre (235 West 49th Street), 85–86
Forty-Niners, The (Kaufman and Connelly), 88
Franco, Francisco, 98, 100, 103
Frank E. Campbell funeral home (1076 Madison Avenue), 116–117, 119
Frazee, Harry H., 87
Fronton speakeasy (88 Washington Place), 58

Gaiety Theatre (1547 Broadway), 83–84
Gardner, Edward E., 81
Garland, Judy, 89, 117
Garrett, John II, 58
"Garter, The," 23
Genovese, Vito, 51
George M. Cohan's Theatre (1482 Broadway), 77
Gershwin, George, 62
Gershwin, Ira, 77
Getting Married (Shaw), 88
Gilford, Jack, 117
Gilford, Madeline Lee, 117
Gillmore, Margalo, 46, 86
Give Me Yesterday (Milne), 88
Grand Central Terminal, 100, 123, 125–126
Grand Hyatt Hotel, 100, 101
Grant, Jane, 45, 49
    as co-founder of *The New Yorker*, 49, 51, 61, 134
Grant, Ulysses S., 21
Greene, Graham, 47
Grossman, Joan, ix, 123
Guild Theatre/August Wilson Theatre (243–59 West 52nd Street), 87, 88

Guinan, Texas, 117

Hale, Ruth, 30, 46, 91
Hammerstein, Oscar, 89
Harper's Bazaar, 23, 65
Harris, Robert, 122
Hart, Moss, 129
Harte, Bret, 70
Harvard Club (27 West 44th Street), 46
Hayes, Helen, 73, 86
Hayward, Susan, 136
Hearst, William Randolph, 43
Hearst (newspaper chain), 103
Hedda Gabler (Ibsen), 81
Heiress, The, 84
Held Jr., John, 126
Hellman, Lillian, 83, 100, 102, 112
    as D. P. executrix, 115, 119
    as terrible person, 115–117, 119–120
Hell's Kitchen, 51, 61, 62
Hemingway, Ernest, 3, 55, 57, 58, 67, 134
    D. P. Hemingway influence, 98–99
Henry, O., 70
    See O. Henry Award
Hepburn, Katharine, 83
Herbst, Josephine, 101
"Here Is New York" (White), 132
Here Lies: The Collected Stories of Dorothy Parker (1939), 13
Herman, Rabbi Floyd L., 124
Himmelrich, Ned T., 124
Hippodrome, the, 36, 47, 48
Hirschfeld, Al, 59, 77, 82, 83, 131
    See Al Hirschfeld Foundation
    See Al Hirschfeld Theatre
Hiss, Alger, 101
Hitler, Adolf, 98
Hooks, Benjamin, 122, 127, 136
Hoover, Herbert, 17, 51
Hopkins, Charles, 88
"Horsie" (1932), 66
Hotel Astor (1515 Broadway), 102–103
Hotel Majestic (115 Central Park West), 28–29

Hotel Volney. *See* Volney Apartments
Houdini, Harry, 48
House Beautiful, The (Pollock), 71, 77
House Un-American Activities Committee, 101, 102
Houseman, John, 74
Hudson River Park, 8

"I Live on Your Visits" (1955), 54
"I Wished on the Moon" (1929), 127
Ibsen, Henrik, 81
"In Broadway Playhouses" (drama column), 70, 126
"Interview" (1925), 39
Iveson, Helen Droste (D. P. niece), 120–122, 128
Iveson, Robert (D. P. nephew), 120, 122
Irish Republican Army, 121
Irvin, Rea, 52
It's a Wonderful Life, 94

Jack and Charlie's (42 West 49th Street), 57–59
Jacob Ruppert Brewing Company, 50
Jersey Shore, 14, 20, 21
    See New Jersey
Joint Anti-Fascist Refugee Committee, 92, 98, 100, 106
Jolson, Al, 70–72
Joyous Season, The (Barry), 97
"Just a Little One" (1928), 33, 53

Kael, Pauline, 54
Kahn, E. J., 54
Kahn, Gordon, 59
Kaufman, Beatrice, 29, 46
Kaufman, George S., 15, 17, 29, 43–46, 52, 79, 88, 94, 117
Kelly, Anthony Paul, 85
Kent, Rockwell, 105
King, Dr. Martin Luther Jr., 1, 105, 119
Kisselev, Mrs. Eugene, 103
Klopfer, Donald, 57
Knickerbocker Hotel, 60–61

Knoblauch, Edward, 78
Krapp, Herbert J., 81
Kriendler, Jack, 58

Labor reform, 4, 5, 89, 94
Ladies of the Corridor, The (Parker and d'Usseau), 83, 86, 87, 115, 116, 136
Ladies Home Journal, The, 65, 113
Lady Beyond the Moon, 81
Lady Gregory (Isabella Augusta), 45
Lady of the Camellias, The, 89
"Lady with a Lamp" (1932), 66
LaFarge, John, 126
La Guardia, Fiorello, 51, 126, 129
Lake, The, 83
Laments for the Living, 11, 13, 93, 135
Lamparski, Richard, 113
Lansburgh, G. Albert, 83
Lansky, Meyer, 51
Lardner, Ring, 88
Lardner, Ring Jr., 105, 117
Latouche, John, 83
Leech, Margaret, 46, 126
Leigh, Jennifer Jason, 130
Leipsic, Nate, 80
Lennon, John, 117
Lenox, James, 66
Lexington Theatre (569 Lexington Avenue), 89
Liberty Theatre (234 West 42nd Street), 75, 76
Life magazine, 32, 65, 75, 79, 134
"Life's Valentines," 75
Little Island (Pier 55), 7, 8
Liveright, Horace, 56, 57
    See Boni & Liveright
Loew, Marcus, 89
"Lolita" (1955), 54
London, Jack, 70
Longacre Theatre (220 West 48th Street), 86, 87, 136
Lord, Pauline, 85
Louard, Janette McCarthy, 124
"Lovely Leave, The" (1943), 11, 64

Lovett, Adele Quartley Brown, 67
Lovett, Robert A., 67
Lowell apartments/hotel (28 East 63rd Street), 66, 67
Luna Park, 47, 48
LVMH (Louis Vuitton Moët Hennessy SA), 60
Lyons, Leonard, 105
Lyric Theatre (223 West 42nd Street), 77

MacArthur, Charles, 41, 60, 62, 73, 134
Madonna, 66
Mafia, in New York, 50–51
Majestic Hotel. *See* Hotel Majestic
Manhattan
 as D. P. subject, 1–4, 10
 Hell's Kitchen, 61–62
 speakeasies, 57–61
 theater district, 72–89
 See also New York City, Upper West Side
Manhattan Towers Hotel (2162 Broadway), 105
Mankiewicz, Herman, 45
Marriott Marquis Hotel, 71, 81, 84
Marston, Ellen Caroline, 123
Marston, Thomas, 123
Martin Beck Theatre/Al Hirschfeld Theatre (302–14 West 45th Street), 82–83
Marx, Chico, 79
Marx, Groucho, 791
Marx, Harpo, 45, 62, 79
Marx, Zeppo, 79
Matthau, Walter, 87
Maugham, Somerset, 75
McCarthy, Joseph, 85
McClain, John, 42, 66
McGraw-Hill building (148 West 48th Street), 85
McMein, Neysa, 45–46, 60, 65, 73, 94
Meade, Marion, 87, 121–122, 130
Medical Bureau to Aid Spanish Democracy, 92, 100–101
Melville, Herman, 123, 126
Mencken, H. L., 47, 58

Mercury Players, 74
Metropolitan Opera House building (39th Street and Broadway), 41, 134
Millay, Edna St. Vincent, 58, 91, 101
Miller, Arthur, 43, 112
Miller, Marilyn, 71, 72
Milne, A. A., 88
Mitchell, Joseph, 54
Monroe, Marilyn, 43, 89, 112
Morehouse, Ward, 109
Morosco, Oliver, 79, 80
Morosco Theatre (217 West 45th Street), 79–81
Morton, Lackenbruch & Co., 6
Mostel, Kate (Kathryn Harkin), 116, 117
Mostel, Zero, 109, 112, 116
"Mr. Durant" (1924), 6
Mrs. Parker and the Vicious Circle, 130
Murphy, Gerald, 40, 67, 94
Murphy, Patrick, 40, 94
Murphy, Sara, 40, 67, 94, 111
Music Box Revue, 86
Mussolini, Benito, 98
"My Home Town" (1928), 131

Nabokov, Vladimir, 53
Nast, Condé, 35, 75
 See Condé Nast Publications
Nathan, George Jean, 87
National Association for the Advancement of Colored People (NAACP), 121, 124, 127
 Baltimore headquarters, 122–124
 Claim ashes (1988), 122, 136
 D. P. bequest in will (1967), 119
National Children's Book Week luncheon, 102–103
National Council of American-Soviet Friendship, 102
National Institute of Arts and Letters (633 West 155th Street), 111–112
NBC, 59, 105
New Amsterdam Theatre (214 West 42nd Street), 74–75

150 | Index

New Jersey
   Birthplace, 4, 19–21, 24, 112
   Hall of Fame, 131
   Literary Landmark, 20–21, 131
New Weston Hotel (34 East 50th Street), 100
New York City
   labor reform in, 4–5
   Mafia in, 50–51
   population (1900–1930), 4
   Prohibition (1919–1933), 46, 49–51, 55
   See also The Bronx
   See also Manhattan
New York Distilling Company, ix, 123, 128
New York Hospital, 66
New York Herald-Tribune, 77
New York Public Library, 66
New York Sun, 42, 64
New York Times, 10, 16, 49, 64, 79, 83, 134
New York Tribune, 37, 64
New York World, 4, 64, 77, 134
New York World-Telegram, 106
New York World-Telegram and The Sun, 109
New York Yacht Club (37 West 44th Street), 46
New Yorker, The
   Baltimore ashes story (2020), 124
   D. P. drama reviews in, 69–70, 73, 75, 81, 88
   D. P. short fiction in, 10, 33, 41, 54, 66, 105
   D. P. verse in, 12, 135
   founding of, 10, 51–53, 61–62, 115
Newhouse, S. I., 54
"News Item" (1925), 39
Nineteenth Amendment, 101
Nineteenth Century, 4, 20–21, 51
Nixon, Richard, 101
No Sirree! (musical revue), 51, 85, 88
Normandie (ocean liner), ii
North American Committee to Aid Spanish Democracy, 95, 100
Not Much Fun: The Lost Poems of Dorothy Parker (Silverstein), 46, 114

O. Henry Award, 11, 41, 93
O'Casey, Seán, 104

O'Dwyer, Paul, 120–122
O'Dwyer & Bernstien (99 Wall Street), 120
Oh Look! (Carroll and McCarthy), 85
O'Hara, John, 53, 58, 67
O'Keeffe, Georgia, 43
Obama, Barack, 122
Olmsted Brothers, 126
Olmsted, Frederick Law, 31
On the Town, 79
One Astor Plaza (1515 Broadway), 104
O'Neill, Eugene, 70, 85

Paley, Babe, 112
Paley, Bill, 112
Parker, Dorothy
   Academy Award nominations, 94, 130, 135, 136
   ashes and urn, 119–130
   birthplace, 4, 19–20
   blacklisting of, 91–96, 102–107
   cynicism and wit of, 13, 21, 35, 98, 130
   death as preoccupation, 11, 12, 30
   death of, 16, 115–117
   dogs owned by, 26, 29–33, 67, 105, 115
   as drama critic, 36–37, 69–89
   early years, 4–8, 19–34
   Federal Bureau of Investigation. *See* FBI
   funeral, 116–117
   legacy of, 16–17, 130–131
   love of animals, 26, 30–33, 67, 105
   Manhattan as subject, 2, 17
   marriages
      Alan Campbell (1934), 10, 54, 59–60, 67, 94–99, 104, 109, 112–115, 135–136
      Edwin Pond Parker II (1917), 6, 10–11, 15, 35, 37, 41, 46, 58, 63–64, 132–134
   memorial garden (Baltimore), 122–123, 136
   miscarriage, 91
   nightlife of, 57–62
   as playwright, 83–84, 86–87, 136
   religious/cultural identification of, 2, 14–15

Index | 151

Parker, Dorothy *(continued)*
  romantic relationships, 41, 60, 65–66
  Sacco and Vanzetti protest, 90, 91, 98
  schooling, 12, 14, 19, 21–22
  screenwriting, 67, 94, 99–100, 112
  short fiction of, 11, 23, 33, 41, 53, 70, 77,
    86–87, 93, 105, 136
  social justice, 97–99, 105
  as songwriter, 127
  suicide attempts, 11, 41–42, 46, 66, 109,
    134–135
  teen years, 22, 29–31
  theater works of, 83–84, 86–87, 136
  will and estate of, 1, 105, 119–121
  women as subjects, 6
  Woodlawn Cemetery grave, 124–130
  words and phrases attributed to, 114
  World War I, 6
  World War II, 92, 94
Parker, Edwin Pond II (first husband), 10–11,
  15, 35, 37, 41, 46, 58, 63–64, 132–134
  Divorce, 11
  Marriage to, 6
Pemberton, Murdock, 48
Penn Club (30 West 44th Street), 46
Penn Station, 124
Peter Pan (Barrie), 22, 27, 71, 73
Phantom Legion, The (Kelly), 85
Picasso, Pablo, 98, 115
Pickford, Mary, 47
"Picture Gallery, The," aka "Oh, Look—I
  Can Do It, Too" (1918), 36
Playhouse Theatre (137 West 48th Street), 85
Plaza Hotel (5th Avenue and Central Park
  South), 43, 111, 54–56
Plymouth Theatre/Schoenfeld Theatre (234–
  40 West 45th Street), 81
Pollock, Channing, 77
Portable Dorothy Parker, The (1944, 2006),
  12–13, 16–17
"Prayer for a New Mother" (1928), 15
Presbyterian Hospital (41 East 70th Street),
  65–66
Prince, Harold, 83

Producers, The (film), 116
Prohibition, 49–51
Proulx, E. Annie, 53
Pulitzer, Joseph, 4, 126
Pulitzer, Ralph, 126
Pulitzer Building (Park Row), 64
Pulitzer Prize, 46, 71, 88
Punch and Judy Theatre/Charles Hopkins
  Theatre (155 West 49th Street), 88–89

Random House Publishing, 57
Red Channels (55 West 42nd Street), 104
Red Head speakeasy, 58
Red House (350 West 85th Street), 29–30
Redemption (Tolstoy), 81
"Résumé" (1925), 39–40
"Revolt of the Intellectuals, The" (Chambers),
  102
"Rhapsody in Blue" (Gershwin), 62
Rice, Elmer, 83–84
Rios, Fernando de los, 95
Riverside Park, 19, 30–32, 35
Robeson, Paul, 105
Robinson, Harry G., 122
Rockefeller Center, 50, 57–59
Rodeph Sholom School, 27
Rogers, Will, 58, 70–71, 75
Roosevelt, Eleanor, 100, 105
Roosevelt, Franklin, 101
Rose Room (Algonquin Hotel), 46
Ross, Harold, 43, 49, 51, 61, 107, 115
  residence (412 West 47th Street), 61–62
Rothschild, Bertram (brother), 24
Rothschild, Eleanor (stepmother), 15, 25–26
Rothschild, Eliza (mother), 4, 7, 20–21, 24,
  123, 127, 130
Rothschild, Elizabeth (aunt), 7–8
Rothschild, Harold (brother), 24
Rothschild, Helen (sister), 21, 24, 26–27, 65
Rothschild, Jacob Henry (father), 4, 7–8, 14,
  20–21, 24–25, 28, 30, 33–34, 123
Rothschild, Martin (uncle), 7–8
Rothschild, Mary (grandmother), 7
Rothschild, Samson (grandfather), 7

Rothstein, Arnold, 51
Round Table. *See* Algonquin Round Table
Roxborough, Mildred Bond, 122
Royalton Hotel (44 West 44th Street), 41
Rudolph, Alan, 130
Ruppert, Col. Jacob, 50
   See Jacob Ruppert Brewing Company
Ryskind, Morrie, 79

Sacco-Vanzetti case, 90–91, 98, 101
Salinger, J. D., 2, 53
Samuels, Art, 45
Sanger, Margaret, 101
Sarafina!, 84
Saroyan, William, 47
Schatt, Roy, 26
Scott, Campbell, 130
Scottsboro Boys, 105
Screen Writers Guild, 94
Second Church of Christ, Scientist, 101
Selznick, David O., 132
"Sentiment" (1933), 23
Seven Year Itch, The, 89
Shannon, Frank, 85
Shapiro, Laurie Gwen, 123–124
Shaw, George Bernard, 88, 91
Shawn, William, 16, 54, 115
Shelton Hotel, 43
Sherwood, Robert E., 36, 43, 45
Shoot the Works (Broun), 77
Shor, Toots, 120
Shubert Brothers (aka Shubert Organization), 48, 81, 84–87
Shubert Theatre (225 West 45th Street), 71
Siegel, Benjamin Hyman "Bugsy," 51
Silverstein, Stuart Y., ix, 46–47114
Simon & Schuster, 57
Slesin, Aviva, 130
"Small Hours, The" (1926), 63
Smalls, Biggie, 117
Smash-Up: The Story of a Woman (Parker and Cavett), 94
Smith, Liz, 121
Smith, Thorne, 35

"Social Note" (1925), 39
"Soldiers of the Republic" (1938), 53–54, 98
Soma, Tony (*see* Tony Soma's), 57–59, 62
Southern Conference for Human Welfare, 93, 100
Spain, civil war in, 52, 54, 91–95, 98–101, 104
"Spain and Peace," 98, 104
Spanish Refugee Appeal of the Joint Anti-Fascist Refugee Committee (23 West 26th Street), 98
speakeasies, 2, 10, 37, 49–51
Speakeasies of 1932, The (Kahn and Hirschfeld), 59
St. Cloud (1466 Broadway), 61
St. Nicholas (magazine), 22
St. Regis Hotel, 60
Stage Door Canteen, 79
Stallings, Laurence, 17, 45, 52
Star Is Born, A (1937), 94
Starr, Frances, 87
Starrett, Goldwin, 46
Stars and Stripes, 44
Steinbeck, John, 102
Steinem, Gloria, 112–113
Stewart, Beatrice Ames, 109, 115, 117
Stewart, Donald Ogden, 17, 45, 109, 117
Stieglitz, Alfred, 43
subway (IRT), 20, 35, 64, 71, 103
suffrage movement, 5
Summit Hotel, 89
Sunset Gun (1928), 11, 13, 57
Supreme Court of the State of New York (60 Centre Street), 106
sweatshops, 33–34
Swiss Alps (restaurant), 65

Tales of a Wayward Inn (Case), 47
Tammany Hall, 4
Tanguay, Eva, 54, 75
"Telephone Call, A" (1927), 17, 65
Tell, Olive, 80
Ten Year Lunch, The: The Wit and Legend of the Algonquin Round Table (Slesin), 130

Index | 153

Tender is the Night (Fitzgerald), 67
Thackeray, William Makepeace, 21
theater district, 43, 69–89
Theatre Guild, 87–88
Thomas, "Professor" Jerry, 126
Thomas, Olive, 74
Thompson, Frederic, 48
Thompson, Kay, 55
"Threnody" (1926), 56–57
Thurber, James, 54, 115
Tiffany & Company, 126
Tiger! Tiger! (Knoblauch), 71, 78
Times Square, 60–61, 72, 74–75, 102–104
Titanic disaster, 7–8
"To My Dog" (1921), 32–33
Tolstoy, Leo, 81
Tony Soma's (speakeasy), 53, 58–59
Toohey, John Peter, 48
Topper (Smith), 35
Town Crier, The (Woollcott), 67
Town Hall (123 West 43rd Street), 101–102
Transcendentalists, 51
"Treasurer's Report, The" (Benchley), 62, 86
Trevor, Norman, 74
Triangle Shirtwaist Factory fire, 33
TriBeCa (Manhattan), 34
Trump, Donald, 101
Twenty-first Amendment, 51

Union Field Cemetery (Queens), 8
United States Army, 6, 43, 62–63, 84
United States Army Air Forces, 94
United States Coast Guard, 58
Upper West Side (Manhattan), 2, 19–35, 62–63, 93, 124, 130
Utica Drop Forge Tool & Die Works, The, 41

Vanderbilt, Cornelius ("Commodore"), 100
Vanderbilt, Gloria, 109, 111–112, 117, 119
Vanderbilt Theatre (148 West 48th Street), 84–85
Vanity Fair (magazine)
    D. P. drama criticism in, 37, 43, 69, 73–75, 78, 81, 84–85, 89

    D. P. job on, 9, 11–13, 54, 62
    D. P. verse in, 9–10, 14, 22, 34, 36
    Staff of, 22, 35–36, 41, 55
Vanity Fair (Thackeray), 21–22
Vaudeville, 36, 48, 54, 75, 77, 82, 89
"Vicious Circle." *See* Algonquin Round Table
Vogue (magazine), 9, 12–13, 21–22, 35–36, 54, 69
Volney Apartments (23 East 74th Street), 1, 104–105, 109–110, 114–116
Volstead Act, 49–51

WBAI (radio), 113
W. W. Norton, 57
waiters' strike (Waldorf-Astoria Hotel), 97–98
Waldorf-Astoria Hotel, 43
    Lobby clock, 97
    Old Waldorf-Astoria, 60
Walker, Madame C. J. (Sarah Breedlove), 126
Wallace, David, 45
"Waltz, The" (1933), 23, 66
Warren, Whitney, 100
Warwick Hotel, 43
Washington, George, 106
Weaver, John V. A., 45
Welles, Orson, 74
Wells, H. G., 91
West End, New Jersey (D. P. birthplace), 4, 21, 24, 112
West, Mae, 71–72
Wetmore, Charles D., 100
White, E. B., 54, 115, 131
White, Katharine Sergeant, 54
White Star Lines, 8
Why Marry? (Lynch), 71
Wilbur, Richard, 83
Wilde, Oscar, 74
Williams, Bert, 126
Williams, Jesse Lynch, 71
Wilson, August, 87–88
Wilson, Edmund "Bunny," 65
Wilson, Woodrow, 49
Winchell, Walter, 75, 104
Winnie-the-Pooh (Milne), 88

Wodehouse, Pelham Grenville "P. G.," 36–37, 69
Women's Committee of the Medical Bureau to Aid Spanish Democracy, 92, 101
women's rights, 5
Wood, Peggy, 46, 117
Woodlawn Cemetery, ix, xi, 2, 30, 123–126
Woollcott, Alexander, 10, 15, 17, 43, 52, 58, 62, 67, 77, 79, 94, 97–98
World Series (1919), 51

World War I (Great War), 6, 10, 43, 79
World War II, 24, 71, 74, 79, 87, 92, 94, 99–100, 102, 104, 112–113

"You Were Perfectly Fine" (1929), 53, 77

Zeffiro, William, 127
Ziegfeld Follies, 71
Ziegfeld Jr., Florenz, 54, 75
Zucker, Albert, 29

About the Author

Kevin C. Fitzpatrick is the author and editor of eight books that are all tied to New York City history. He was awarded the Apple Award for Outstanding Achievement in Non-Fiction Book Writing by the Guides Association of New York City for his two recent books: *111 Places in The Bronx That You Must Not Miss* (Emons) and *World War One New York: A Guide to the City's Enduring Ties to the Great War* (Globe Pequot Press).

Kevin launched dorothyparker.com in 1998 and founded the Dorothy Parker Society the following year. He has written and edited four books tied to the Algonquin Round Table and Dorothy Parker.

He is the shepherd (president) of The Lambs, the oldest professional theatrical organization in the United States. Kevin is a licensed New York City sightseeing guide and has been leading literary and history tours of New York for more than two decades. He is a veteran of the United States Marine Corps and has a passion for military history.

Kevin and his family live on the Upper West Side of Manhattan.

Visit his sites, FitzpatrickAuthor.com and BigAppleFanaticsTours.com.

BOOKS BY KEVIN C. FITZPATRICK

111 Places in The Bronx That You Must Not Miss

World War I New York: A Guide to the City's Enduring Ties to the Great War

The Governors Island Explorer's Guide

The Algonquin Round Table New York: A Historical Guide

Under the Table: A Dorothy Parker Cocktail Guide

A Journey into Dorothy Parker's New York

As Editor

Dorothy Parker Complete Broadway, 1918–1923

As Co-Editor

The Lost Algonquin Round Table:
Humor, Fiction, Journalism, Criticism and Poetry from
America's Most Famous Literary Circle